C000072368

MOVE FAST. BREAK SHIT. BURN OUT.

THE CATALYST'S GUIDE TO

WORKING WELL

MOVE FAST
BREAK SHIT
BURN OUT

TRACEY LOVEJOY
AND
SHANNON LUCAS

LIONCREST
PUBLISHING

COPYRIGHT © 2020 TRACEY LOVEJOY & SHANNON LUCAS
All rights reserved.

MOVE FAST. BREAK SHIT. BURN OUT.
The Catalyst's Guide to Working Well

ISBN   978-1-5445-1578-6 *Hardcover*
       978-1-5445-1577-9 *Paperback*
       978-1-5445-1576-2 *Ebook*

TO YOU, CATALYST, AND TO EVERYONE
WHO EMBRACES YOUR FIRE.

CONTENTS

cat·a·lyst: *noun, singular*

a person, thing, or event that quickly causes change or action.

con·stel·la·tion: *noun, singular*

a group of stars forming a recognizable pattern.

Catalyst Constellations: *noun, collective*

a movement that helps Catalyst changemakers sustain their energy so they can maximize their impact and work well.

INTRODUCTION

Innovators. Changemakers. Entrepreneurs. Intrapreneurs. Catalysts.

One of these things is not like the other.

That is to say, each of these types of people can make a whole lot of change happen in the world, but within any group of innovators, changemakers, entrepreneurs, and intrapreneurs, there is a subset of people we call Catalysts. Those who have a deep-rooted need to create positive change.

Among Catalysts, there is an unmet need to be seen and valued for who we are and how we show up in the world. We know because we feel it too.

We move so fast that we lose people. We can break shit without intentionality. And all of that can lead to burnout—frequently.

Catalysts feel a deep sense of drive toward a better future state. We can't help but see potential change and set it in motion, wherever we are. We're energized and driven by it.

There's a speed to our action that tends to outpace the people around us, for better or worse. And we are driven to create that change whether we are starting our own thing or in an organizational context—our catalyticness is who we are.

When someone asks us what a Catalyst is, the short answer is: it's a person who takes in lots of information, sees infinite possibility, and can't stop themselves from moving into action.

The longer explanation is why we're writing this book.

You might have read a dozen books on innovation and change management already. We all have. Some of us—Catalysts—already have an innate drive to make change. It's in our DNA. We *are* change.

So where are the books on how to manage *ourselves*?

If you've felt this way your whole life, you aren't weird or crazy—and more importantly, you aren't alone. You're a Catalyst. So are we. Welcome.

FINDING MY PEOPLE: TRACEY LOVEJOY

After I left my job in research, leadership, and in-house coaching at Microsoft, I decided to become a leadership consultant. At the end of a year of fearful paralysis, my own coach suggested I do research to figure out who I'd most like to support. When I analyzed the patterns of my former favorite clients year over year, the data that emerged blew my mind. I typed up a frenzied, seven-page synthesis and sent it over to my very confused coach.

I tried to explain—the attributes I found didn't match any population I could think of. And I loved working with them, not just because they showed up well and were open to change, but because I could relate to them on a deeper level. The significant traits that they shared seemed to only belong to this group of people—to us—and we didn't broadly share any other backgrounds or demographics. Traits such as:

- They set audacious goals in their personal and work life.
- Many goals they set are about making positive change in the world around them.
- When they share those goals, they are scared to say them out loud. They know they were huge goals, and they can't seem to help themselves.
- By the next time we speak, they often can't remember the goals, because they've already been integrated into their lives.

The list went on, and when I compared it to niches identified by the International Coaching Federation, there just wasn't a category for my people.

Around that time, I met with a client at the old Tully's down at the beach, and they shared a revelation: "I'm a Catalyst. I get things started, and I get things done."

Neon signs flashed in my head: that was it! That was the descriptor for my people.

I was eager to learn more, so I set up a few interviews with existing clients. At first, I was asking questions to help me develop my service offering, but by the second interview I realized I was hearing information that I had never heard before. During my time working in the technology field, I had read myriad books on the process of innovation. But now I was hearing about the skills, pain and patterns of stumbling blocks of the people driving innovation in a richness I had not yet encountered. That led me to launch a series of in-depth qualitative interviews across 2016 that took me on a journey of discovery.

And while the data collection itself was a journey of expectation, emotion, and new realizations, as soon as I started posting about my findings, more people reached out. They told me they felt as if I were talking directly to them. As if I saw them as no one else had. As if I were helping them make sense of their experiences in a way they had never experienced before. I heard even more stories of pain and loneliness—of having always felt weird, and of how empowering the research felt for them.

We still hear this kind of feedback, over and over, to this day.

In addition to primary research, I dug into existing literature to see what existed for me and this group of likeminded people I'd found. I was particularly interested in how many Catalysts there might be to have quantitative data to correlate to my growing qualitative data. Two pieces that were foundational for me were *Leadership Agility* (Joiner and Josephs, 2006) which discusses categories of leaders that have mastered the level of agility needed to be consistently effective and avoid burnout in today's turbulent global workplace (including one category they label Catalysts—it was great to see others drawn to that word as well), and 2015 research by eg.1 consultancy in the UK that identified corporate employees they call "Game Changers."

Using these as a proxy, we estimate Catalysts to be somewhere between 5 and 11 percent of the workforce. Looking across the research and my career to that point, the numbers felt right—perhaps even more optimistically than what I'd experienced. At Microsoft, many people had positive intent toward innovation but still pushed hard against change. Even among a world-renowned group of techies and intrapreneurs, I could look back and see that Catalysts were a small percentage of that pool.

They were the ones who thrived on discussions around change, even when they realized we couldn't manifest them all. They were the ones who saw possibility as a form of play, rather than getting annoyed or overwhelmed. I had been drawn to those people—my people—even then.

By 2017, I had a powerful research base, rich knowledge of Catalysts, and a brand-new business partnership with Shannon.

Today, working with Catalysts feels like I've tapped directly into my sense of purpose. As if I am bringing knowledge forward that was waiting to be unearthed. As if this information is coming *through* me, rather than it being mine at all.

Catalysts aren't just parts of the innovation machine that can be replaced once they wear out, though that is certainly how they were treated during many of my years at Microsoft. Too often, organizations replace inconvenient, disruptive, out-of-the-box changemakers with people who are younger or hungrier or more malleable to the existing systems.

No, taken care of well, Catalysts only get better and more effective at creating positive change.

That's who I'm showing up for in my work, my daily presence, and in the heart of this book.

If I can help the most effective and talented changemakers be better at tackling the world's problems, then I am helping the world be better at an order of magnitude I never could have dreamed.

FINDING MYSELF: SHANNON LUCAS

I have always felt different. In high school, I started a recycling program—but I didn't stop there. I ignited a few close friends on the issue who, in retrospect, also happened to be Catalysts. They helped me develop a marketing campaign, and that helped us galvanize a broader group of students who hadn't previously cared about sustainability at all.

In college, I saw a need to increase funding resources for students on scholarships. That problem could only be solved by getting involved with student government, so I became the senior class president.

I have always moved through the world thinking "What's the next problem and how do I fix it?" And more than that, "Who can help me amplify this for maximum impact?"

Even in much less purpose-driven work, when I was a single mom just paying the bills, I always found myself on the cutting edge of technology. I wanted to know what was out there and how I could use it to make things better around me.

My first sigh of relief came with an innovation role at Vodafone. It felt life-changing—like there was finally a role for me.

Though it wasn't without its challenges, it was my dream job. In building the Innovation Program, I knew that we had to create a movement of like-minded change agents throughout the organization. I created the Innovation Champion program, which started with a ragtag group of eight positive troublemakers from around the world and eventually grew into a CEO-sponsored, gamified, multi-level global program with over one hundred Innovation Champions. But even as these volunteers raised their hands and worked with their management structures to get permission to be part of this elite squad, not all of them showed up the same. It was the same ten people who religiously joined every call, made their way through all five levels of certification and always leaned in, hard. I kept thinking that there was something more I could be doing to increase engagement across the community.

While others in my team seemed to be able to leave work at the office, I couldn't create any distance at all. Failure on the job felt personal. Criticism of my work felt like criticism of me. If my ideas were bad, then I must be bad. Each setback sent me deeper into burnout, without me even realizing what was happening. I was increasingly allowed to align my sense of Purpose with my day job: helping smallholder farmers across Africa develop credit scores to get access to capital, working with the world's largest companies to create more sustainable supply chains, changing how people worked so they could be more fulfilled. The more aligned my work became with my vision of the positive changes that needed to be manifested in the world, the harder I worked, despite increased resistance. I lacked a sense of community outside of my core group who really understood my challenges, both professionally and personally. Work became a drain instead of a source of energy.

My health suffered. My relationships suffered. And I had no idea why.

As I traveled all over the world running innovation workshops with the world's largest organizations, I kept an eye out for other likeminded people, looking for leaders in similar roles as mine. The struggle of being a highly motivated innovator only grew, and I craved a support group; a safe space where others like me could share our challenges, laugh about the craziness, and cry at the hard battles fought and lost, sometimes at great personal expense. In response, I started a hand-selected group for intrapreneurs called the Global Intrapreneur Salon. My intention was to co-create a movement where people who joined the group would each take a turn hosting a call to share thought leadership and bring in external speakers or new recruits. But soon, it became painfully clear that even in this carefully curated group of people I thought were more like me, many in this group didn't lean in and take action the same way. The more changemakers that I met, the more alone I felt. It was just me and my work, and even that was losing its joy.

It wasn't until Tracey interviewed me as part of her Catalyst data collection that I finally got it. She had a name for me—a description that finally made everything make sense. And she didn't just help me self-identify—she helped me understand my process and find tools that would help me thrive. And not just me—the people in my network that I could now label appropriately as Catalysts stood out from other change agents, and our biggest shared problem was burnout.

I had already contemplated hosting a weekend getaway for the Salon to rejuvenate. I deeply needed it, and knew others did, too. So in typical Catalyst fashion, I immediately decided to create a space for us, and Tracey was on board. There on the coast of Northern California, with plans for a hot tub, good food, good wine, and good people, Catalyst Constellations was born.

THIS IS OUR TIME

As quickly as we'd like to change the world, the world is changing around us that much faster. The concept of an increasingly turbulent and chaotic world, where the pace of change is ever accelerating, has been gaining awareness and traction over the last few decades.

In the late 1980s, at the intersection of cutting-edge leadership research and the military's desire to create a new security understanding about the post-Cold War reality, the term VUCA (Volatility, Uncertainty, Complexity, and Ambiguity) was introduced.

VUCA provided a new context for strategic foresight and insight, outlining both systemic and behavioral shortcomings experienced by organizations that have not internalized or been able to plan for VUCA realities.

Since the initial coining of the term, we have experienced the massive global adoption of the internet, connecting people and things, now generating 2.5 quintillion bytes of data a day.[1] This has accelerated and deepened our VUCA reality. By the early 2000s, VUCA as a term became more widely used across all disciplines, no longer just in military circles, in response to the fact that massive global trends like digitization and

---

1   For perspective, that's 2,500,000,000,000,000,000!

climate change were already altering the way organizations needed to operate. It meant that organizations had to start acknowledging that disruption could come from new players never before considered or even imagined.

As we have all experienced firsthand, VUCA reality is no longer theoretical or on the horizon. It's here now, not only in the form of global pandemics, massive economic shutdowns, racial justice movements, and global climate crisis, but also in the opportunities we have to create more regenerative systems, more inclusive societies, and radically changing ways of working. A "business as usual" culture is no longer sustainable. Leaders who hope to carry their organizations to the future will need to adapt. Enter VUCA Prime.

In 2007, Bob Johansen, founder of the Institute for the Future, presented a response framework that he coined VUCA Prime: Vision, Understanding, Clarity, and Agility. These qualities are the antidotes to a VUCA world, giving us a tangible way to identify the skills required to not only survive uncertainty but to lead through it.

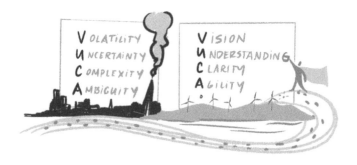

We believe that vision, understanding, clarity, and agility are skills that Catalysts inherently possess. Well-supported Catalysts, in particular, have the potential to emerge as superheroes in an increasingly VUCA future.

But no superhero is without their blind spots, and for the Catalyst, there are quite a few.

Whether or not an organization can name VUCA Prime or quantify our specific strengths, we are often invited in to create change in a changing world. Later, when the same people who brought us in start backing away from us or withdrawing support, it can feel like gaslighting or like some weird reality shift happened under our feet. As the change gets more imminent, they might even attack the output, or us directly, while we're left wondering what happened and where we went wrong. This can be a core experience for Catalysts and a key factor in burnout.

The sense of betrayal and self-doubt you feel in those moments isn't imagined—it's a function of life as a Catalyst. Tilting toward VUCA Prime and leveraging vision and clarity instead of getting lost in uncertainty and ambiguity helps to extend the runway toward burnout a bit, creating more space for you to embrace and leverage your superpowers.

As Catalyst Constellations has expanded from our initial retreats and into a global network, our goal has been to help Catalysts understand themselves—superpowers and blind spots alike—so they can more powerfully change the world.

This book is built on the same foundation that helps Catalysts begin to thrive when they work with us directly: We'll create clarity around who you are as a Catalyst, the nuances of your process, and what it's like for the people who work and live with you. We'll help you find deeper connections—first through the stories of other Catalysts, and then through tools and resources that help you to connect with people who see and understand you. And most importantly, we'll explore what rejuvenation practices look like and how they support and sustain your work.

It's never going to be easy to be a Catalyst. You probably won't be able to avoid burnout for good. But you will feel seen. You'll feel more powerful and confident in who you are. You'll understand why people love your work sometimes and are threatened by you at others. You'll learn how to set boundaries and discover better ways to push new frontiers.

We won't tell you how to make change, but we will help you move fast without losing people, break shit with intentionality, and lessen the intensity and frequency of the burnout cycle. We aren't going to tell you to stop working toward change—we're going to help you work well.

FOR THE QUESTIONING CATALYST

Catalysts aren't limited to one industry, role, gender, race, geographic locale, career stage, or any other demographic designation. We are simply not limited at all.

We see possibilities around us, and we step directly into that swirling vortex of opportunity. Our ideas never stop coming, we never stop taking action, and we never stop learning, pivoting, and moving forward. And it often happens all at once, creating change in one fluid motion that others think of as magic.

It kind of *is* magic.

But every magician has their secrets, and we're going to unlock ours.

We'll share stories from other Catalysts who weren't sure if they belonged, and who might still be unsure. We'll see others who have been deeply burned out, hoping for a way to not be a Catalyst anymore.

We'll see the clear attributes that define a Catalyst and their unique way of approaching the world. Only you will know whether or not those attributes apply to you and to what degree.

If we could look at a sliding scale of catalyticness, Tracey might be on a more cautious end of it with her research and stage of life, while Shannon would be on the far end, feeling an intense drive for change in all areas of her life.

There are very few hyper-catalytic people in any given organization, and that's ok. Maybe you're on the quieter end of that scale, or maybe you're burned out, or maybe it all feels too big to claim as your own. That's all ok, too. You don't have to know anything right now. Self-awareness and clarity are a process, and this book is a great way to explore.

Just know this: If you find that you're a prolific changemaker or a skilled innovator but *not* a Catalyst, the tools in this book will still be beneficial. It's good to know how to rejuvenate. It's good to know how to orchestrate better and have more empathy for your colleagues.

But if you *are* a Catalyst, those tools are going to feel like a lifeline. Hang onto them. If you need to, reach out to us. Because you've got a hell of a life ahead of you, and we want you to be equipped for every second of it.

PART I

THE CATALYST DEFINED

CHAPTER 1

AM I A CATALYST?

When Catalysts get together—and sometimes when we're on our own—we are often perceived as intimidating. We make connections that others don't and run with ideas that others merely float. We often forget that rejuvenation doesn't always look like work, and that our identity can exist apart from the change we're currently trying to make. We move *fast*, and that can be hard to keep up with. So when Catalyst Constellations opens up a retreat or class or gathering of any sort, someone usually shows up with questions.

Am I *really* a Catalyst? And if I am, what does that say about me or the work I'm doing? Am I doing enough to "count?"

Our good friend Chelsey is a prime example. When she came to our retreat, she was an individual contributing researcher at Google. She didn't think of herself as an innovator on the front lines. Surrounded by Catalysts like Abby, who at the time was working on a business model structured for women, or Georges who had a book with Harvard Press in progress, Chelsey admitted that she felt a little out of place.

She saw herself pushing new ideas and trying new research methods but always within her container of the world. For a little while, she questioned whether that qualified her as a Catalyst. Was she still a Catalyst if she saw and made change but still stuck to her role? In our minds there was no doubt—she took in information within her role, built corresponding visions of how she could help Google improve their offerings and moved to action to push toward those visions. Being a Catalyst is a way of being—not a particular size of project or impact.

Sometimes, it's energizing and empowering to discover language that describes who you are and connects you to others who think like you do. Other times—if you're closer to burnout, or if you express your gifts as a Catalyst outside of the executive's suite, or if you've internalized years of negative messages about yourself—it's harder to get on board.

For the questioning Catalyst, we have both good news and bad news for you. The good news is that this isn't about making change on a global scale, though that does happen for some of us. While we've found that as Catalysts learn the skills to thrive and hit their stride, they see their own scale increase almost by definition—but that scale is still relative to each individual.

The catch is, if you're a Catalyst, you don't hide well. Even for the introverts who keep a lot of their process internal until it's time, or the people like Chelsey who are happy sticking to their role as long as possible, there's still something different about the way you approach work compared to your peers. This isn't about stacking up merit or accomplishments. This is about how you think, act, and move through the world, no matter what corner of the world you find yourself in.

DEFINITIONAL TRAITS OF CATALYSTS

Our work with Catalysts emerged when we identified recurring patterns that certain people exhibited—the kind of people that a coach loves to work with. They had goals that included ways to create positive change, expected to meet them, and often moved right along to the next goal while forgetting about any fear around the first. It wasn't about the goal so much as always moving forward, always making things around them better.

The research began with people within Tracey's network or extended network, or who reached out after her first article about Catalysts was published online. Each of them self-identified as Catalysts, and each participated in an in-depth qualitative interview via phone or video chat. The traits and patterns that emerged formed the basis of our understanding of Catalysts. As our work expanded into retreats, screenings, group sessions, and surveys, the initial research was confirmed time and again: Catalysts constantly take in information, see lots of possibility and a better future state, and have a drive to transform toward that future. Then, as Catalysts move into action toward that future, they naturally iterate based on the new information that action uncovers.

While we do transform situations, that transformation will look different for every Catalyst in every situation. You might transform the way your daughter sees the world, the way your company is structured, or the way your department approaches research—or some combination of all of it. The key differentiator for a Catalyst is that we see the potential for transformation all around us, and we're likely to act on what we see.

SUBCONSCIOUS DATA COLLECTION

Catalysts have told us, "I'm comfortable operating in the fog, with 40 to 70 percent of the information backed by strong intuition," "I powerfully lead from the front," and "I trust my intuition."

What they don't say (because they don't often know it) is that their *strong intuition* is actually a thorough data-collection mechanism that eliminates a great deal of the unknown.

Catalysts process data at lightning speed. We absorb information quickly and easily from conversations, experience, research, emotional intelligence, subconscious observations, and overt data. Then we process it systematically and contextually, often without realizing we're doing any of it at all. It can feel as subtle as intuition or as intense as a "storm"—quickly cycling through data collection that inspires or informs a vision, then acting and iterating on that data over and over until more concrete data is formed.[2]

Typical leadership around change involves a much slower process of vision, orchestration, and implementation of the original vision. Catalysts don't follow that timeline. After the storm of data produces a vision, we can't unsee it. The solution becomes so clear that we jump right into manifestation, sometimes unaware that we are going to iterate on the original solution many times before it becomes real. The less intentional we are about this process, the messier it can be—especially to an outsider who expects a more linear progression.

---

2   Keep that cycle of Vision, Action, and Iteration in mind, as it will become a key way to understand the Catalyst Formula in the next chapter and throughout the book.

CONSTANT POSSIBILITY AND CLEAR VISIONS

The information that we take in allows us to see lots of possibility. A better future is always in sight, even if we haven't fully registered that we've come to that vision—and even when we forget to say it out loud. Many non-Catalysts are able to consume a lot of information, but not everyone comes up with new ideas and new visions from that information. Catalysts, on the other hand, can't stop themselves.

LOTS OF IDEAS

A VISION OF HOW THE WORLD COULD BE

More than a process or a skill, this is a way of being in the world and interacting with it. There is a sense of always having something else to do, always working through one thing to get to the next. The possibilities when we're "on" never end.

Catalysts see lots of possible ways to improve the world around them and a drive to make that a reality. The less aware we are of what's happening here, the more likely we are to stumble in our communication of it. Because people who aren't Catalysts haven't experienced that data storm or don't have the ability to piece together the puzzle, we can struggle to find the words (or patience) to bring them along with us. We see a dimension that they haven't experienced yet. This pitfall is not definitional for Catalysts, but it tends to be a painfully familiar experience for most of us.

AN INHERENT DRIVE TOWARD ACTION

It's not enough for the Catalyst to take in data at lightning speed, process it contextually, and put the puzzle pieces together to shape a vision. Creating that transformation becomes an almost physical necessity. If you see the possibility, then you see the opportunity, and you're driven to move into action.

This drive toward change comes across as a purpose for existence. We manifest change because it's painful not to. We see all of the moving parts that will make the vision become a reality, and we can't leave it alone until it's done—or at least ready to hand off to someone else. It's in your DNA to see situations, processes, and organizations improve, and you can't imagine sitting back and letting those changes go undone.

AN EXPERIMENTATION MINDSET

Because we engage with the world through a lens of betterment, we aren't rigid in the change we hope to manifest. Constant forward momentum requires an experimentation mindset. With each action that we take, we create more data and feedback to help the next action be even more effective. Our actions aren't right or wrong—they are simply necessary. And feedback is a natural part of that process—a forward movement towards manifestation.

This mindset creates extraordinary resilience in the Catalyst and continues to set us apart. For the changemakers who take in a lot of information and tend to synthesize it into a vision, not all are driven to action, and even fewer are able to adapt that vision fluidly as new information becomes available.

BONUS TRAITS: RISK, AMBIGUITY, PARTNERSHIP, AND INTUITION

The above traits tend to be core to nearly every Catalyst we've worked with. But there are a few others that crop up, at least in how we present to the world. When we question whether we are Catalysts, seeing ourselves through others' eyes can help us come to a new layer of self-awareness.

When others describe Catalysts, they tend to see us as having a sense of risk tolerance, a belief we are comfortable in ambiguity, the feeling that we push our partners, and the appearance of a strong intuition.

While we tend to believe that others simply missed the data that eliminated risk, we are often told we're risk tolerant. To the Catalyst who has already sorted out the possibilities, potential outcomes and pitfalls, and the most reasonable path forward, it doesn't feel risky to us. *They* might need yet another analyst report, but *we* feel ready to move forward.

Also, we're sometimes perceived as being comfortable with ambiguity, but really, we've just learned that constantly tackling new challenges comes with a level of ambiguity, like it or not. We don't necessarily feel comfortable, but we come to accept it.

Some Catalysts may in fact be risk tolerant and comfortable with ambiguity, but in most cases that is an outside perspective that's formed when someone hasn't internalized all of the information that we have.

Another perception issue happens in the way we interact with our partners at work and in our personal lives. Becoming a better version of ourselves is inherent in our process, and we often expect others to constantly see areas of personal change and act on them as well. We assume everyone wants to optimize everything just like we do. *Of course* you'd want to know you aren't doing that great. *Of course* you want to do that better. *Of course* we all want everything around us to always improve.

We have impossible standards for ourselves, and we hold high standards for those around us, often without empathy or even awareness of the way that impacts others. Catalysts tend to say things like, "If I go into a project, I want to make it a success. I see the moving parts to make it happen. Why can't they? Don't they *want* to improve?"

As we'll see in the next chapter, and as you've likely experienced already, constant friction becomes a spiral of iteration that drains us emotionally and energetically. It can become a source of trauma that affects every facet of our lives, including how we view ourselves.

Finally, the Catalyst's process happens so quickly that it feels like an unconscious ability we don't know how to explain other than to call it intuition. Some Catalysts are deeply intuitive—we tend to see an overlap between Catalysts and HSPs, neurodivergence, and other atypical ways of being in the world. But whether our intuition is real or perceived, that way of looking at the world begins to feel so normal that we tend to think everyone thinks like us.

PAUSE WITH TRACEY

The first time I connected with a sense of purpose, I was twenty years old and doing research at the Library of Congress. Right then, I knew I was meant to help people be happy. I also knew I had no idea what that meant and no real way to change my trajectory to make that happen. So, I went on with my work. When I moved on to do research at Microsoft, I left that voice whispering about purpose tucked into the back of my mind.

After I had my first child, I was promoted to manager and embraced the gift that it was to be able to stay close to home more often.

It was also a gift to be responsible for people.

Suddenly, people were in front of me with whom I could have direct impact. I could see their strengths and reflect back their worth and concerns and values. A few years after that, I was introduced to coaching—as well as the opportunity to leave my stable job with good healthcare and take the leap toward my purpose. I could become a coach full-time. I could help people be happy.

On a resume, my trajectory is jagged and has big gaps. But it was exactly what I needed. Without taking time as a researcher, then getting to know people as a manager, I wouldn't have developed the experience and skills I needed to be a coach.

What my twenty-year-old self thought about helping people be happy is not at all what I know to be true today. More accurately, my purpose is to help people see themselves and stand as comfortably in their strengths as possible. In those moments, I get to watch my clients' anxious energy and discomfort and fear fall away, like they are the eye of the storm, or Neo navigating the Matrix. It doesn't matter whether the term Catalyst helps them reach that point or whether they just need to hear from someone else that they are a superhero, too—self-awareness unlocks something deeper and more meaningful than "happy."

If you find one thing within the pages of this book, let it be that sense of purpose, awareness, and calm. Catalyst or not, you deserve to stand in your strengths.

THE DEEPER VALUE OF SELF-AWARENESS

As the picture of a Catalyst becomes clearer, you might still find some internal resistance to owning that label. This is normal. The more divergent an idea, the more work we have to do to warm up to it and see ourselves in it. In our experience, something extraordinary happens when a Catalyst steps into their power—in other words, we aren't always as intimidated by other Catalysts as we are by our own potential.

Knowing and owning your strengths and working through your weaknesses can be equally difficult. It requires looking back to properly count your wins, as well as acknowledging how you contributed to some of your previous challenges.

The research is still out on whether a Catalyst is born or made. No one is going to issue you a Catalyst-card if you make enough change, and no one will revoke your status if you don't meet the invisible criteria. You already know if some of it is ringing true. You've found yourself out in front of change time and again, wondering why no one else can see it. You feel that shift that happens when the puzzle pieces lock into place and you're ready to jump into action. You've been the magical visionary that everyone loves, and you've been the scapegoat when change got hard.

Without being willing to self-reflect, the tools in this book won't move the needle. But it's worth facing the darkness in order to make it to the light. The change you want to make in yourself, your relationships, and your world is worth the pain to get there, and *that's* why you're here.

Honestly, you just want to be able to work well, because it's more than just work to you.

You want it so much that you get frustrated when others aren't on board, because you see just how much better the world could be. You've probably even been feared, disliked, and perceived as arrogant because of that frustration, when all along you just wanted things to be...better. *Why don't they get it?*

You've felt crazy, overwhelmed by the weight of your ideas, and unsure why you're only able to pursue a fraction of them. You've felt responsible for the emotional lift of the whole organization, draining you in both hours worked and energy spent. And you've chosen it because the thing you hope to manifest has become an all-consuming passion.

If you're not ready to claim your unique abilities as Catalyst for yourself, then do it for the sake of the change you want to see in the world. Self-identification is about our own confidence, yes, but it's about empathy as well.

When we write-off our unique process as automatic or something that everyone can do, we come to expect too much of the people around us. Why can't they move faster, see the connections, or just make the change already? Because they literally don't operate that way.

Once we identify Catalyst superpowers and the details of our dark side, we can begin to bridge the gap between the way we work and the way others work, then step into something better for us all. Only through honest self-reflection, will you be able to apply those learnings to yourself and your specific current context.

It should be noted here that we are often asked how to know whether an organization, team, or spouse even *wants* a Catalyst in their life. How do we know where to go and whether we'll be accepted there?

Unfortunately, this isn't a question that we can ever fully answer. There isn't a definitive checklist that will give you permission to stay or to leave. It's far too personal and dependent upon each unique situation. This is why self-awareness and mindfulness are so important.

We'll talk a lot about the supercharging impact rejuvenation practices can have on your journey as a Catalyst, and this includes mindfulness, self-awareness, self-compassion, and empathy. By cultivating mindfulness, we begin to see ourselves more clearly (self-awareness), with kindness (self-compassion), and with a clearer understanding of the experience of others and how we impact them (empathy).

Using these tools of rejuvenation, alongside the others that we'll present throughout the book, we can become more aware of our energy levels and how to better sustain them.

Is your energy tank empty? Can you take a step back and honestly evaluate the likelihood of success in your current role? Only you will know the answers to these questions.

But understand that it's easy to lose sight of the "truth" of a situation within stories we tell ourselves in the speed and fury of slaying dragons to create change. Mindfulness helps us develop a new, more detached, objective clarity about the reality of our situation that leads to better ways of working within it.

With that said, psychological safety is a serious need for everyone, Catalysts included. If you've found yourself lacking an advocate or champion, if your partner or organization is unwilling to lean into change, or if you are burned out so much that nothing gives you energy anymore, it's time to get serious about making internal or external changes. And the most important place to find acceptance is within yourself.

CATALYSTS HAVE PATTERNS, NOT TEMPLATES

Different environments and scenarios will present different opportunities and challenges for Catalysts. If you're the boss, you may bump into fewer issues with disruption, but you'll also leave more people behind. We see high incidences of Catalysts in roles where their ideas and drive for change are welcomed, such as entrepreneurs, consultants, designers, and researchers, as well as with titles like "Head of Innovation," "Head of Sustainability," and other natural disruption roles. However, a Catalyst can learn to thrive in almost any circumstance. We work with Catalysts that work in compliance, government offices, human resources—we are everywhere.

When you're a mid-sized cog in a big wheel, you'll run into different kinds of burnout than someone running a company and motivated by change. If you're transitioning from one role to another, there is a great deal of potential to work toward your audacious goals, but that comes with a great deal of fear. The energy exchange will vary from circumstance to circumstance, and so will the potential outcomes.

Four positions come to mind that are important to differentiate, because they can tell us so much about Catalysts in various stages. They are the leadership level of a large organization, the individual contributor within an organization, the entrepreneur, and the Catalyst who is building whatever will come next.

Incidentally, each of the Catalysts we're about to highlight in the following story vignettes have already shifted from one stage to another, sometimes multiple times.

We move from leadership to consultant to individual contributor and back again, driven by the next challenge, which may be packaged up in different forms in different moments. The burnout and trauma that we experience can necessitate a quick exit from one position out into a transitional space and then into something new. The threat we sometimes pose to an organization can make that happen involuntarily. In any case, this exercise in categorization is less about finding yourself in a particular profile and more about seeing the ways catalyticness shows up in various contexts.

With that said, let's look at each stage through the lens of specific Catalysts, and the way their challenges and opportunities varied.

LEADING IN A LARGE ORGANIZATION

 Van sat with her hand at her side when almost everyone else's was in the air. We had just asked who could relate to feelings of imposter syndrome, and she and one other Catalyst simply could not.[3] Her track record at the leadership level of large organizations speaks for itself, and she knows it—even when she steps into new organizational contexts.

In fact, when Van considers her ideal roles, she prefers to solve ambiguous problems rather than maintain something already established. The combination of a position of power with the freedom to choose how to make that happen gives Van space to create the vision as it needs to be, rather than working from previous constraints. She does this through an exercise she calls listening tours, where she takes in as much information, opinion, and concern as she can before creating a unified vision that will serve the new purpose.

In one especially fulfilling role, Van accepted the appointment of Vice Chancellor to drive the workforce mission of California Community Colleges—the largest system of higher education

---

3   The other Catalyst was Virginia, whose incredible story shows up later in the book.

in the country, with 113 institutions back then—without having been a higher education administrator in her past. She started the role during the Great Recession, with workforce budgets cut as severely as half and foundations walking away from investments in the state of California entirely.

Her goal moving into that environment was simple and clear: find ways to help students. With that level of clarity, she was able to double the discretionary funds, then raise them again, from $100 million at first to over a billion dollars by the end of her gubernatorial appointment.

Her advice for other Catalysts in positions of leadership is just as clear: find ways to listen to and accept feedback. The space she creates between herself and criticism of her work allows her to step into new roles with less fear and inhibitions—it's not about her, after all. It's about the change she's working to create.

THE CATALYST IN LEADERSHIP

What we love: the clear demonstration of our value; lessening of imposter syndrome with more data points for success; freedom to control and impact an entire system; dreaming big; being in charge. While no Catalyst will move through their changemaking process without resistance, it's less likely to stop someone who's in a high level of power. The ability to dream big and then back it up with actual implementation is alluring for the Catalyst who is able and willing to step into leadership roles in larger organizations.

Where we struggle: visibility of failure; consequences of failure for others; boredom at the top; difficulty starting over without taking a step down; loss of personal time and rejuvenation space; loss of identity apart from the role. The tradeoff for all of the influence and control is deeply personal. Leadership at this level requires so much of us that we can easily lose ourselves and all of our rejuvenation practices in the process. CEO and high-level leadership Catalysts require extra intention, in creative ways, to avoid burnout levels that scale with our rise through the ranks.

CREATING CHANGE AS AN ENTREPRENEUR OR SOLOPRENEUR

 Abby is a graphic designer and graphic recorder (whom we have to thank for the fantastic images in this book). We connected with Abby when we first hired her for that skill, and she identified as a Catalyst right away. It was her catalytic ability to process information quickly and connect the dots that made her so great as a graphic recorder—which looks like listening to a speaker, processing what they're saying, putting a structure in place for it, and capturing it graphically all in the time it takes most people to just hear the speaker. It's an incredibly powerful gift, and she's been invited all over the world to share it.

Abby realized early on, back when she was studying at Berkley, that she wanted to work with people she loved to be around. And that's exactly what she did. In typical Catalyst fashion, she found a few people she loved to work with and set off into the world to create something new with them. In every step of her entrepreneurial journey—including the difficult decision to pivot back to solopreneurship during and after the pandemic—Abby has been intentional and thoughtful about the decisions she makes for the company. Instead of CEO, she chose the title of Founder and WIC (Woman In Charge).

When she has people, they work four-day workweeks—and not ten-hour days, either. She constantly thinks about equity of the staff, new growth opportunities, and potential new uses for their graphic recording services.

Being able to define who she wants to be in the world allows Abby to play and experiment rather than adapting herself to existing organizations. Even the decision to shift back into solo work was one she could make because of the flexibility that entrepreneurship allows. There are definite tradeoffs to be made around security and separation of identity and work, but Abby's commitment to rejuvenation practices helps her preserve the personal space necessary to take advantage of the creative space her role facilitates.

THE CATALYST ENTREPRENEUR

What we love: autonomy; choosing our ultimate role and title; flexibility; alignment with passion and purpose. As an entrepreneur or solopreneur, Catalysts can literally create the change we want to see in the world. Resistance shows up, but not in the form of an organizational roadblock—we create the organization. And if and when we want to pivot, we do. The flexibility of entrepreneurship matches our energy in a way that other roles do not.

Where we struggle: workaholism; lack of boundaries between work and personal life, especially when the work aligns with purpose; financial uncertainty; imposter syndrome; no organizational shield or brand supporting you. The same flexibility and purpose alignment that allows us to breathe can also allow us to get in way too deep. No one is there to remind us to stop or take a break—and like the CEO or high-level leader, we may not have the luxury of taking a break. Without financial security or intentional space between ourselves and the work, we can get lost in it and dip into burnout, fast.

FINDING YOUR PLACE AS AN INDIVIDUAL CONTRIBUTOR

 Alex recalls a former role as a business analyst with mixed feelings. Early on, she had a supportive mentor whom she felt comfortable bringing ideas and concerns to. As a Catalyst—though she didn't have a term for it at the time—she saw paths to change intersecting and arcing from multiple angles. She thought critically about every action, not to *be* a critic but to ensure the success of critical systems. And with her mentor as her boss, she could speak up in those scenarios without being shut down for pointing to things outside of her swim lane. But no good thing lasts forever, and when that boss was promoted out of her network, the replacement wasn't so understanding.

The changes didn't happen overnight—more like a slow burn that was difficult to detect. Piece by piece, Alex and her colleagues lost agency, creativity, and empowerment when it came to building solutions. Being able to flex and explore had made her job exciting, but it wasn't until those freedoms were taken that she realized just how important they had been. In fact, even then she shouldered the blame for how drained and demoralized she felt at work.

When you lose safety nets as an individual contributor—especially before you're aware of what it is to be a Catalyst in that context—it's like the rug gets pulled out from under you. It's disorienting and not uncommon to wonder whether your magic has just run out. Self-doubt creeps in, especially if you're young or more junior in your career. You work more hours, take on more tasks, and do whatever you can to prove yourself and regain a place of safety and trust. But as Alex discovered when her doctor warned that work was diminishing her health, you'll pay the price for that approach, without any return.

Eventually, she realized that she couldn't work in a way that all parties would consider valuable, and she made the choice to shift to another role. To hear her tell it now, the choice came way later than it should have. Alex encourages Catalysts to spot those warning signs early and seek out a mentor, boss, or team who will support you and your superpowers.

THE CATALYST INDIVIDUAL CONTRIBUTOR

What we love: aligning with organizations we love; being part of an effective team; financial security. When being an individual contributor works, it really works—we can really enjoy having the freedom to explore without being responsible to lead any of it to fruition. Get on the right team, and you can grow and thrive as a Catalyst in this role.

Where we're challenged: not having permission to act on obvious visions; getting smacked for being outside of your swim lane; losing your support people suddenly and without warning; staying on too long, hoping things will get better. The energy for change that we bring into every space we occupy is not always appreciated on junior or contributor levels. We can present as threats to the organization, or at least to established power, and that can quickly become unsafe, exhausting, and traumatic. Be aware of who you are as a Catalyst and how you're perceived, and constantly look for people and structures that will support and protect you.

Georges' early stages of creating change in the energy division at GE was filled with excitement, even heady-mania, with C-Level sponsorship not just from within the division but from the mothership. He had a bold new vision, a Catalyst partner, and support from key senior Catalysts across the organization. But he felt he couldn't put time into more purposeful paths—a book he is writing and an incubator he wanted to create—alongside his day job. After some time, he made the hard decision to quit his job and step into a transitional phase.

When we met him in 2018 at one of our retreats, he had already made that pivot toward focusing on sustainable energy solutions in Lebanon, running a nonprofit on the side, and grappling with where his focus should be directed. Afterward, he secured a book deal with Harvard Press, working through the research that he'd done while trying to support the change he knew he needed to see. That's when Georges rejoined the Catalyst community with one of our online experiential courses—to reconnect with the visioning process, to renew his clarity about where he was now headed, to reignite Catalysts skills and supercharge his multiple projects, and to reconnect with the community.

Since the course, Georges worked with dozens of Fortune 500 companies to explore how they can best engage with climate tech startups. Through the Catalyst network, he has connected with a Catalyst who is also working on a book and facing similar challenges. They have partnered up to motivate and inspire each other, and his book is well on its way. Even better, he's no longer alone in what can be a chaotic and frustrating phase for anyone, much less a Catalyst who sees all possibilities and has to choose a path forward.

THE CATALYST WHO'S BUILDING WHAT'S NEXT

What we love: the space to think about what's next; no one to limit your impact or direct your focus; time to rejuvenate; space to consider your purpose. This can be a stimulating time for Catalysts, where we are free to shape a brand-new vision for the future and where we belong in it.

Where we're challenged: financial insecurity; open-ended choices; judgment from others and ourselves; imposter syndrome. Without an accountability structure or clear direction, we can feel untethered and a bit lost. It's nice to be able to move at your own speed, but when you aren't sure where to go, speed can get us stuck.

THE "CATALYST" TITLE ISN'T THE POINT

You don't have to resonate with the word "Catalyst" to feel a sense of connection to the experience we're calling catalytic and the community we've created around that experience. At the end of the day, the opportunities and challenges that we face as Catalysts might take on different faces, but underneath it all, we're working from the same mechanisms, benefits, drawbacks, powers, and blind spots. We experience the same drive for change, the same impatience with our constraints, the same pitfalls, and the same fantastic potential, even when the context changes.

Being a Catalyst isn't about the role that we're in or the type of change we're making—as Van demonstrated, most of us will pivot many times over the course of a career. We are multifaceted people with a range of strengths, weaknesses, needs, and opportunities. Like Georges, we can gain clarity around what we need in order to decide our next steps effectively. Like Abby, we can forge connections with others who can support us and our vision, and who will give us the space we need to maximize our opportunities. And, like Alex, we can come to recognize warning signs that we're on a path toward burnout, then regroup in a more supportive environment.

Whatever you choose to call it, becoming aware of your traits as a Catalyst and intentional about your process makes the scale of change possible—and sometimes inevitable. You might not get a deal with Harvard Press or a billion in funding, but you certainly won't be able to stay the same. For the Catalyst, we'd argue, it's not in our nature to remain stagnant anyway.

Remember Chelsey, who wasn't sure if her work at Google "counted?" She saw herself on the edge of change but always within the container of her world, while everyone else seemed fearless and always driving new innovation in big and important ways. That is, until she hit her own inflection point.

Both she and one of her direct reports experienced pregnancy discrimination at Google, and she could not be silent about it. Not only did she leave her role, but she wrote a letter that went viral and opened a legal case against the company. She threw herself into this effort in every way, made the news, and ultimately changed pregnancy discrimination legislation in Washington.

We don't reference Chelsey to say that you'll one day be in the public eye, *like it or not*. We reference her because she, too, wondered if she was really a Catalyst. It didn't matter what external boxes she checked or what her role looked like before. It was just who she was as a person. She couldn't help but make change, especially once someone in her direct care had been affected. Her question quickly shifted from, "Am I a Catalyst?" to "Is this worth it?" and "Can I keep going?"

The path of the Catalyst is not the one most trodden, but it's not entirely abandoned either. If what we've said so far about Catalysts has resonated with you, keep reading. You're not alone.

Keep reading even if you have doubts.

Keep reading even if you aren't sure you meet an arbitrary minimum threshold of work.

Keep reading *especially* if you're weary and would rather not be a Catalyst anymore.

There is no pressure to perform here, only tools that support the real you and the work you love to do.

AM I A CATALYST? CHECKLIST AND SELF-SURVEY

☐ Do I feel driven to do things to make the world around me better?

☐ Do I frequently piece together information quickly and see a path to action?

☐ Do I sometimes feel crazy because a solution or path seems obvious to me, but people around me don't see it?

☐ Do I sometimes overwhelm people around me with all the ideas I have?

☐ Do I sometimes overwhelm myself with all the ideas I have?

☐ Do I often challenge the status quo or get referred to as disruptive?

☐ Do I get frustrated by people who talk a big game, but then don't act, because results matter as much as the idea itself?

☐ When tackling a challenge, do I try different approaches and figure out which is most effective as I go?

☐ Does the term Catalyst just feel like it fits?

CHAPTER 2

THE CATALYST'S JOURNEY TOWARD BURNOUT

Catalysts show up in the world as powerful, sometimes magical forces for change. Even when we're a bit messy and uncoordinated in our efforts, the overall impression is one of energy and action. We see opportunities that others don't, and we're compelled to act on them in order to make the world better. We're always embarking on something new, whatever that looks like in our own unique context. We live in the space of discomfort and the unknown, much more than anyone else does.

But the external view is only a piece of what's happening. What does it actually *feel* like to move fast, break shit, and burn out—over and over again?

This is the Catalyst's journey. Our highs are higher, the lows are lower, and we cycle through them more often, creating a constant rollercoaster more than a definite arc. Like the archetypical hero, after the depths of burnout hopefully emerges a deeper understanding of our gifts and an ability to face the world anew. But unlike the archetypical hero, before we've had a chance to process what happened, the next quest for change has our attention.

Catalysts report regular cycles of tackling new challenges, then plummeting into burnout. We move quickly through the excitement of a new challenge to the peak of possibility, then sink into a cycle of iteration and resistance that causes burnout. And soon (sometimes too soon) we're on to the next surge of excitement as we try to puzzle out the next new solution.

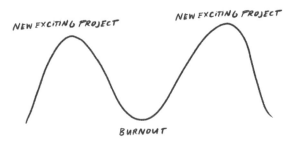

Unfortunately, the energy gained from a new discovery can only last so long. In the day to day, any number of factors can and will shape the reality of your experience. These include how intensely catalytic you are, how supported you are in your organization, and whether you stay long enough to see the change fully manifest. Because our highs are higher and our lows are lower, and it's all happening at a greater frequency than anyone else, we have to be more intentional about the practices that sustain us in that cycle. We frame this as a routine of consistent rejuvenation. It's what enables us to continue the work that we're so passionate about, in spite of our tendency toward unsustainable energy use.

This process is similar to the intensity of childbirth. After it's over and we've recovered, we seem to forget the challenges of the experience completely. We find new energy in what we're going after next and head off down the cliff once again.

More accurately for our context, because we don't love the tedium of driving projects through to the final details of completion and that stage gives us no energy, we move on to the next thing without fully recovering from the last.

While no story is the same and life is never perfectly predictable, there is great benefit in tracing typical Catalyst patterns and then learning how others are more successful in maintaining resilience and agility along the way. That is our objective in this chapter: to look beyond the surface of the Catalyst's journey and see the underlying pattern that, without self-awareness and rejuvenation, drives us to move too fast, knocks us down when we break existing structures, and ultimately leads us to burn out. Once we have the clarity of how we operate when we aren't mindful, we'll explore tools that will allow you to choose a different, more sustainable energetic path.

CYCLES OF ENERGY GAINED AND LOST

Before we get into the tools and tactics that can facilitate our process of change, let's isolate the key stages of the Catalyst's predictable journey into burnout: the mania high of a new challenge, the decline and deceptive energy boost in resistance, the drop into burnout, and what's needed to recover, reach an impactful upside, and lengthen the runway before the next time we bottom out.

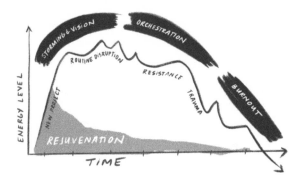

MOVING FAST IN EARLY STAGES OF CHANGE

We see the potential for improvement in everything from the way our departments run to the layout of a bookshelf in the corner of a colleague's office. We notice the way the line could move more efficiently in Starbucks, how Tuesday meetings could be more effective, and what our kids could be doing better every second of the day. The seeing is constant—it's when we zoom in on one of those problem spaces that things start to heat up. The more complex the problem, the more it takes to puzzle together a solution, the more energy we can create.

This stage is best described as mania—not in a clinical sense, but for how truly physical the experience can be. We know that a solution is possible, it just has to snap into place. It's right on the tip of our tongues, and we don't want to do anything else until it's clear. We might not even realize how much time we're devoting to thinking about it. Like being in an internal state of flow while going about the rest of our day, or like soaking up the honeymoon phase of a new relationship, our brains and bodies thrive when we're putting the pieces together.

We can also call this a storming phase, where we're on high alert, more open to data than usual. Whether it's a line in a movie or a line on a spreadsheet, no form of input is overlooked.

Mostly, we get positive energy in this stage from the excitement of delving into a new challenge—although it's not always all positive. Before the vision is complete, we can be plagued with doubt gremlins: *Am I really up to this? Am I good enough? Is it actually solvable?* For problems that we're determined to solve, that anxiety boils around the energy of potential, and that sense of mania builds until a solution snaps into place: "That's *it*! I've got it!"

The key for this emotional stage is to utilize self-awareness to budget that energy out with mindful intention. It's often during this first mania that it feels fine to skip some of our personal energy regeneration practices (going to the gym, seeing friends, meditating) because we're flying high. We don't even realize how much we're giving up, as long as it feels like we're gaining energy from envisioning the change.

If we don't pay close attention, we can lose those habits all together, and it will ultimately contribute to burnout.

As we'll see, it can be easy to view tackling resistance or pursuing "side quests" as sources of energy because of the sense of mania that something new can trigger. Catching ourselves in that moment and refocusing our attention where we'll *actu-*

ally get support and create forward momentum directs our energy in a much more effective way.

MEETING RESISTANCE WHEN WE'RE BREAKING SHIT

Our energy is on a steep incline in the early stages of change. We're building and building as the problem space becomes clearer and clearer, then when we reach the peak with a vision that we're ready to enact. For a little while, there's an energy boost there, too. Action is our ultimate output, so we're more than ready to get the solution in motion. But we don't often have others there at the peak with us, ready to move forward. When that happens, resistance begins to pull us back down.

To coordinate a group of active, willing co-conspirators, this often looks like repeating the vision seventeen different times in as many different words as you can think of to as many stakeholders as you can until you don't want to talk about it anymore. You believe in the vision that snapped into place, and you desperately want to bring everyone along.

The act of orchestration—doing what's necessary to conduct the orchestra of moving parts necessary to make the change come to life—can be a serious blind spot for Catalysts. In that desperation, we can move so fast and break so many of our colleagues' existing systems and familiar frameworks that the people around us can't keep up. That's when the *smile-and-nod* kicks in, and we get verbal agreements to action that never come to fruition. It's when we left the mocked-up vision on their desk but they act like they haven't heard of it before. It's when the people who brought us in to make the change start backing away.

Interesting challenges are magnetic for Catalysts, no matter where they come from. So for a little while, the resistance itself can feel like a problem to solve. We try different presentations, call back to previous conversations, get that confirmation, and then try again.

In our research, Catalysts have said they like to "solve puzzles," "take on wicked challenges," and "unfuck big things." We are detectives, puzzlers, and untanglers. But we can get distracted from our main vision when a shiny new problem—such as untangling resistance—is right there in front of us. The bigger outcome is still there, and we know that we're going to get to it, but the million broken pieces in front of us that we think we need to fix can distract us and pull our energy and focus away.

This is the most destructive part of the cycle. The longer we focus on the broken pieces that resistance keeps creating, the fewer chances we have of finding our way back up to the initial vision. We often start to act as if the resistance is the new problem and throw our manic energy at that, without stopping to really unpack why the resistance is there.

Was the vision clear enough? Did it contain enough wins of the necessary stakeholders? Did the team understand their role in it? If we're honest with ourselves here, we probably skipped a lot of steps along the way that could have brought people along more effectively. And if we missed them in early stages, chances are we'll continue missing them as we iterate around their resistance.

What's worse, because we typically lose our rejuvenation practices in our pursuit of those manic energy sources, it's hard to get back to the stillness and empathy required to unpack where we are and how we got there.

Once the brain is triggered into a severe stress response, it's difficult to slow or undo the process that follows. Buried deep inside the limbic system of the brain, the amygdala takes control any time we're stressed out or afraid. This tiny little piece of the brain creates the most emotional, reactive, fear-activated neural connections. Amygdala-driven, limbic responses are often quick reactions, disconnected from our prefrontal cortex where all of our processing and rational decision making happens.

When we are not regulated, we are no longer making rational decisions that we can trust. If we are in a state of resilience and rejuvenation, we can self-regulate enough to respond well. We stay in touch with the prefrontal cortex and give less power to reactivity and fear.

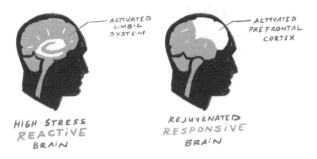

In other words, the best way to minimize burnout is to manage your own self-regulation. This is important to know even in cases where you're choosing to step into situations with a one-way energy drain that will likely lead to burnout—you truly cannot show up the way you want to without mindfulness practices and self-regulation.

When we lose sight of the practices that give us resilience, regulation, and rejuvenation, it's easy to miss how frenetic our energy is. It actually causes people to pull away instead of lean into the problem solving and barrier removal with us. And if we're not careful, that one-way energy drain will eventually empty us completely. That's when we find ourselves stuck in burnout—along with everyone we dragged in with us.

ISOLATED, DRAINED, AND BURNING OUT

To be driven by change is not to simply enjoy it or prefer it—it is part of our very nature. When we're driving toward the potential of change, there is a sense of being in alignment with ourselves. The energy isn't superficial or fleeting. Especially when the change creates something significant in the world, it is a deep and fulfilling sense of power, in an almost spiritual sense.

You can see, then, how painful the equal and opposite sense of burnout might be. A rejection of our work feels like a rejection of ourselves. A loss of energy in the change space becomes a loss of energy in every aspect of life. Knowing how much potential our work holds—not just for the result, but for our own fulfillment—we often sink deeper into that work in an effort to find that feeling again. There's an element of addiction. Just one more hit and we'll be back on top.

Without identifying the spiral of iteration and resistance that can happen at this stage, we can eventually become drained of all passion, purpose, and sense of self.

We haven't seen Catalysts *set out* to sacrifice their marriage or relationships for their work, or lose their true selves in the midst of a project. It happens without us realizing it. The early stage is so exciting and fulfilling that it becomes conflated with self-care, purpose, and everyday necessities.

I don't have time to go out with the girls this week, but I'll catch them next time.

Saturday morning golf is still on, but I'll have to catch a rain check.

Date night isn't feasible this week, but that's part of marriage. We'll get back on track.

I just traveled for eighteen hours—I don't have to go to the gym today.

Somewhere down the line, what had been regular routines aren't actually a thing anymore. Time gets away from us without even knowing it.

Understand that the same drain on energy is happening whether we feel it or not. If we're skipping pieces of our lives that makes us who we are, we're losing something. We just don't notice what we've lost until fighting resistance takes away every last bit of energy that we had and there are no rejuvenation habits or practices left to replenish us.

We don't notice it until our health suffers, our relationships fall apart, or we jeopardize our positions out of exhaustion and reactivity.

The most common sign of burnout is when we say, "It's hard to get out of bed and go to work." It's an early sign, and one that we often ignore far too long. When we push past that point, serious damage can be done. We stop sleeping well. Our relationships become strained. We wind up exhausted all the time without knowing why or how to fix it. Eventually, our health suffers and the work becomes impossible.

Burnout is difficult for anyone, and not unique to the Catalyst. In 2019, the World Health Organization (WHO) added it to its International Classification of Diseases—or ICD-11, a diagnostic tool for medical providers—as a recognized disorder.[4] We see burnout concentrated in the Catalyst community, by nature of the way we work and view ourselves within that work.

When the change you're trying to create feels like a physical extension of yourself, the distance required to protect against burnout is lost. When we begin to lose interest and energy as burnout sets in, particularly if we disrupted relationships and routines for the sake of that work, we can experience a sense of shame and grief. We might reach a point where we don't want to do the work anymore and don't know why we lost that energy but feel unable to talk about it with the same people we previously shared so much of our enthusiasm with. The same physicality that makes the early stage mania so fun and energizing pulls us down in later stages. Without distance between ourselves and what we're manifesting in the world, we are pulled more deeply into the highs and lows of changemaking.

Sometimes, a new challenge will present itself, and we'll get a boost of energy that masks the damage that's been done.

---

4   Interestingly, burnout has not been yet accepted into the American Psychiatric Associations' *Diagnostic and Statistical Manual of Mental Disorders* (Fifth Edition). The divergence between what the global community sees as problematic and what Americans accept as normal is telling.

When we don't know how we got so low before, we aren't sure how to avoid it next time, and the cycle carries on.

The Catalysts who thrive the most, reaching burnout less frequently and for a shorter duration, have a strong sense of routine. They create distance between themselves and the work, holding the rest of their lives as a sacred piece of themselves that is not reliant on the energy of changemaking alone. Their relationships, hobbies, and self-care form a buoyant protective layer that keep the Catalyst afloat when all other support structures fail.

PAUSE WITH TRACEY

As a coach, I frequently work with people who are trying to decide whether it's time to find something new. By the time they get to me, unfortunately, they are so far along their journey toward burnout that finding something new can feel next to impossible. Their sense of personal value has usually been questioned, if not attacked, to the point that stating their value or putting it onto a resume feels incredibly difficult. They're slogging through the emotional molasses that is a burnout journey—and often, they don't even realize it.

When you're that far down the curve, nearing or lost in burnout already, you've been solving for resistance for so long you may not have slowed down to see the toll it's taken on you. You've been using a shovel to help with a broad sense of resistance instead of a screwdriver to sort out the details of the true problems, and before you know it, you've dug a trench.

I want to share with you what I've shared with many burned out, exhausted, tearful clients over the years:

We all make mistakes, especially when we're eagerly working toward something big in the world. But mistakes don't mean you're broken.

The language found in this book will mirror what's found on self-help shelves—mindfulness, meditation, self-compassion, almost tipping into the realm of spirituality. That isn't because we work in self-help. It's because we see you and how worn down you've gotten. We see how you've pushed too hard and been ignored and beaten down too long.

There is a detoxification process required to acknowledge the pain that you've experienced and the toll it has taken before you can rebuild toward something new. Take your time within the pages of this book. Reach out to us for community and support. Look up, however slowly and gently you need to, and face the circumstances you've been working so hard to change. Then take a deep breath and know that you're not alone. You're not stuck there forever. And you are absolutely *not* broken.

THE CRASH TOWARD BURNOUT

Circumstances that make us feel unsafe—such as threats to our livelihood and income, or an ongoing sense of gaslighting—can be experienced as trauma. In chapter 7, when we look closer at rejuvenation for the whole Catalyst, trauma specialist Jenn Harkness explains how these experiences couple with burnout to create serious personal damage, and what we can do to begin to heal and circumvent it. But one of the first steps toward safety is to leave traumatic situations as soon as possible.

Catalysts frequently ask us how to know when it's time to leave, and there is no easy answer. But there are practices and support structures you can put in place to help see your situation more realistically.

Our natural tendency is to see any challenge as something to solve for, which does give us a sense of energy. But in cases where we lose our sense of the ultimate vision or are ultimately never going to make headway, that false energy boost only drives us into an iterative spiral.

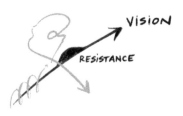

Observation from a bit of distance between yourself and the work can give you a fresh perspective on situations that energy had been masking. Try to observe interactions to notice if they are taking an extra toll on you and get curious why people are behaving in new ways. Usually, it is out of fear of something. If you can see the fear and name it, you are more likely to help them overcome it. If you can identify together what your resistors are struggling against and how you might have inadvertently contributed to the situation, you can then answer the most important question: Is it fixable?

If it's not, then it's time to leave.

Unfortunately, we don't always have perfect choice about the organization that we're in or our role within it. Sometimes, your job is your job and that's the end of it. But even in a less than ideal environment, we can still take steps to protect against burnout as much as possible.

And listen, if you're young and just now starting your career, pay attention early. Shape your life and career in a way that you'll be able to pull the parachute and get out when you need to. The more financial freedom you have, the more room you'll have to explore new options and pivot if the time comes.

TAP YOUR SUPPORTERS, INCLUDING YOURSELF

Before we get to the later chapters filled with tactical tools that make this journey possible, there are four underlying support structures that we've seen in Catalysts who experience burnout less frequently and with less intensity than the rest of us. They are a consistent commitment to rejuvenation, self-compassion, the people you surround yourself with, and the empathy you hold for them. We've seen how rejuvenation can create the kind of space necessary to remain responsive under stress and resistance, but we also need the compassionate support of ourselves and from our community to hold that space.

When our key supporters lose faith in us, it's easy to lose faith in ourselves. We turn a critical lens inward, hoarding evidence of our shortcomings without seeing any of the upside. We lose the audacity of the original vision and begin to spin a story laced with *shoulds* and failures. These messages can be especially amplified for anyone on the margins or at intersections. When you've been told all your life that you don't belong in the system—you're not the right color or gender or age or shape or personality—the messages find a place in your brain and don't want to let go. Then, when you're invited to change a piece of that same system, those old messages will inevitably show back up, shaping your view of yourself and the world.

Self-compassion allows you to give yourself the room to learn, fail, grow, experiment, and be the wonderfully unique change-maker that you are, no matter what anyone has said before.

Self-compassion is bolstered when we have compassionate people around us, too. When we lose our advocates in the workspace and begin to feel targeted, burnout is close at hand. If we've also lost our connection to partners and friends in the time that we were consumed with the energy of the fight, the isolation can become crushing.

Hold your friends, family, community, mentors, and coaching connections sacred. They can offer compassion, help us create distance, and provide a boost out of the pit when all else is lost. They can remind us of our superpowers and magic—the unique gifts that only Catalysts have.

THE NECESSITY OF EMPATHY

There isn't a universal response to Catalysts. We are neither universally loved nor universally hated. Instead, we can think of a distribution curve of change agents that puts Catalysts on one end of the extreme, a larger range of people moderately comfortable with change in the middle, then the most resistant population on the other end.

Like the innovation adoption curve, which models how new concepts or ideas gain acceptance and spread throughout society, Catalysts will encounter similar levels of acceptance or resistance based on people's comfort with change.[5]

---

5   Everett Rogers, a professor of communication studies, built a theory around how, why, and how quickly new ideas are spread in his published in 1962 book *Diffusion of Innovations*. Our adapted model shows how Catalysts will often be early adopters, reminding us that we have to help others toward adoption, rather than assuming they are already there.

In other words, there will likely be at least a few people around you who are as thrilled about change as you are, and at least a few people who cannot tolerate what you're doing to their world. In the middle, you'll find a range of interest, doubt, and concern.

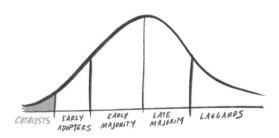

If you have control over the teams you work with, consider the innovation curve and how that team might respond to iteration and plans in flux. While there is a place for people who want homeostasis and will resist every change we present, that place is probably not on your direct team. Those resistors are often vocal about their resistance from the beginning. You know who they are and that they aren't going to adapt well. It's the bulk of people in the middle who you'll need to bring on board, and that's when resistance can eat up iterative energy.

Regardless of their relationship to you, change is difficult for everyone, and we are walking bundles of it.

While it's certainly true that Catalysts suffer from the lack of support and even downright aggression that we may receive as we try to manifest our vision, we must acknowledge that we may simultaneously be unwittingly and unintentionally causing similar stress in others. As we imagine how amazing it would feel to have genuine, unshakeable support throughout the Catalyst journey, we must also bring our skills of empathy to imagine what it must be like for non-Catalysts to work with or for us.

Wrapping your attention around change can damage interpersonal relationships in sometimes lasting and painful ways. Cultivating empathy for the people living and working with us helps us to not only work well with and around others, but to work well in general. Repairing our relationships with others, or being more proactively empathetic moving forward, can help soften our eager presentation into an invitation to change rather than a bullet train that can't be stopped.

It is helpful for Catalysts to remember that every change, even positive ones, can trigger grief for people, and they need time to work through that emotional journey to embrace a new way of being. The Change Curve, based on the stages of grief from psychiatrist Elisabeth Kübler-Ross, illustrates that people need to emotionally work through any change. While we may excitedly and off-handedly suggest a new and better way of being, we can inadvertently be triggering sadness for those around us.

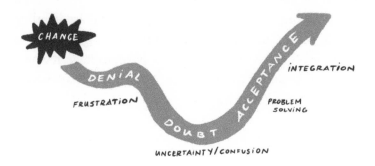

We can be experienced as demanding and never satisfied. The feedback we offer in our unending pursuit for improvement can be experienced as critical, even when delivered compassionately, simply because we constantly see how things can be better. Co-workers can fatigue from the fact that we often overlook the positive feedback for the sake of expediency. The constant moving of the goal can make it feel like they can never possibly achieve success.

Our speed is unrelenting, we work around the clock, our standards impossibly high, we forget to dot Is and cross Ts, we can be overconfident in our vision to a point of arrogance, and we get easily frustrated when we have to repeat ourselves or things are moving too slowly.

Sound familiar?

There are more layers to consider here, too. For example, if you're partnered with another Catalyst or workaholic, you might both be on disparate journeys through mania and burnout. Or your own journey may have multiple arcs that interact with each other.

When we showed the energy curve to our hyper-Catalyst friend Georges, he said, "Just imagine if you are juggling two or three Catalyst projects at different stages. If one of the projects is at a lower point of the burnout stage, it would impact your ability to work on the other ones. That's what's been happening with me."

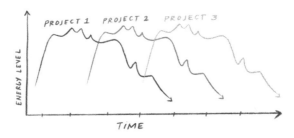

This is why self-awareness and empathy are crucial to both our success and in limiting our experience of burnout. It's important that we look in the mirror and reflect first on where we are on a journey, how that impacts our energy, and how we might be coming across even to those people who are most excited to go on the change journey with us.

By cultivating mindfulness practices, we can create a stronger ability to sense people's emotions and the space we need to be able to respond to potentially challenging situations without reactivity. Slowing down and being a bit more contemplative lets us more fully recognize what our supporters (and sometimes even our detractors) need from us to get onboard and become an active proponent and implementer of the vision. Empathy helps us develop insight into the "wins" for many of our different stakeholders, which will both inform our vision to achieve more goals across the organization and create a higher likelihood of success with more supporters bought in.

In other words, a little empathy and mindfulness can go a long way in accelerating a Catalyst's success.

When we experience resistance, it can be an opportunity to get curious and lean in with empathy rather than momentum at all costs. This frame creates less of an energy dip, by simply using the emotional intelligence that we already have.

REJUVENATION AS THE ANTIDOTE TO BURNOUT

The more frequently burnout pulls us down, the more limited we are in the way we can impact the world. Even when our work aligns with our purpose (or at least doesn't interfere with it), we are completely supported, and the energy extends for prolonged periods of time—burnout is always a risk.

We won't promise a path to eliminate burnout, because we aren't sure that's possible for a Catalyst. Anyone burning this hot is bound to reach their limits, and if you turn off that side of you for any amount of time, the energy required to hold back your natural drive toward change will create its own kind of exhaustion.

Instead, our goal is to make a longer runway before burnout hits, and to lessen intensity once it does. The support structures we just mentioned are a way to do that. The self-awareness we're creating by identifying what it is to be a Catalyst and owning our strengths and blind spots is another. With more consciousness, we gain more control. As we come to know ourselves more closely, we can identify key stages of our work cycle and begin to create that much-needed distance. We see the differences between solving challenges and spiraling around resistance. We learn what we don't want and look for things that give us true, sustainable energy.

But the only way to hold all of those supportive practices and still enable the work we're doing is to establish and prioritize a routine of rejuvenation. Self-awareness, compassion, and self-care allow us to direct all of our energy for a better future inward as well. Care for ourselves as whole, entire humans is vital—especially as we move quickly through change, disrupt organizations, and push ourselves beyond our limits in service of a bigger goal. It makes the work *the work*, separate from who we are and what we're doing in the world. And that distance is invaluable.

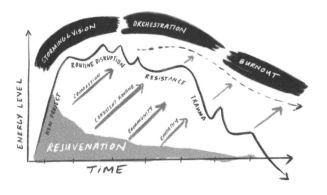

We want to be very clear here: You, Catalyst, *are* a hero. *You're a fucking superhero.* You hold incredible potential. But we're not going to promise a clean journey with a clear ending. We're not going to throw you a few tools and watch you fly away triumphantly. This world is built of Kryptonite, and you're going to have to hold onto your superpowers in spite of it.

That's the power we want to create for you. Not to avoid the struggle and get to the ending but to get back up and do it again, with a little bit less personal sacrifice. To know both your strengths and your shadow, and use them to make significant things happen in the world. To know just how incredible you are, how perilous your journey is, and to travel it well.

And, dare we say it, to maybe have a bit more fun along the way.

The great power of a Catalyst is that we see the path to a brighter future. Of course that brings resistance. Of course that drains our energy. And of course, now more than ever, it has to be done.

CHECK-IN ON YOUR BURNOUT JOURNEY

☐ When you reflect on your history, do you see a pattern of burnout?

☐ Are you able to identify what contributed to your periods of burnout?

☐ When you are experiencing high stress are you able to self-regulate and be responsive?

☐ How often do you use empathy to consider your impact and the impact of your ideas on others?

☐ How easily can you tap into self-compassion?

☐ Do you have regular rejuvenation practices in place?

☐ Where on the journey to burnout are you right now?

☐ Am I sacrificing my sleep routines or health in any way?

CHAPTER 3

THE CATALYST FORMULA

This is the part of the movie where the soundtrack falls away, diving through an impossibly deep bass scale until the last note resonates in your chest and stays low. It thumps out the rhythm of a slowed pulse. Time has changed, and audience members of all ages know that something *wicked cool* is about to happen.

The heroes have banded together to face the enemy.

They're clearly outnumbered—the odds are impossible.

But just one hero is the focus now. We know it's them because they're ready for battle. A flick of the chin to crack their neck, ear buds turned on, a stick of gum popped in their mouth, a smirk. *It's on.*

The other heroes might know what's coming, but the bad guys don't have a clue.

Off our hero goes, moving in normal time as everyone around them slows to a near freeze. They travel from one end of the room to the other, making changes at every point. Sometimes it's as big as a planted bomb or a knife in the back. Sometimes it's a redirected fist or a flicked-away bullet. The little tweaks and shifts they leave in their wake mean nothing to the bad guys just yet...but our hero knows exactly what they're doing. They saw what needed to be done, knew they were the only ones who could make it happen, and took off without a moment's hesitation.

When their work is complete, the scale reverses and the soundtrack returns to its original adrenaline-fueled electronica, this time in a key that indicates victory rather than impending doom.

Time is back to normal, and the consequences of our hero's actions are revealed all at once. The bad guys all fall to the ground. Faces have been punched. Bullets have missed their mark. Items have been stolen. And our hero gives us one more smirk before moving on to the next stage of peril.

This is the power you possess, Catalyst.

We can't go invisible, though we sometimes hope to fly under the radar. We don't have super strength, though we sometimes try to carry more weight than we should. The truth is much simpler, and more extraordinary, than all of that: we're doing the things that every organization values in a changemaker. We're just doing them faster than anyone is ready for.

We see changes that need to happen, and we don't hesitate to set them in motion, adapting as quickly as needed in order to reach our objectives. We have a clear vision, a path toward action, and the capacity to iterate as obstacles pop up. When we're done, we're ready to move on to the next challenge.

But because we're moving "faster than a speeding bullet" every step of the way, what we do often looks like magic. To the outside observer, we're there one minute and gone the next. It takes a concerted effort for anyone to see exactly what we're doing as we do it—including us. We move on instinct, then *keep* moving, rarely pausing to acknowledge the remarkable power we have and superhuman amount of work we've been able to accomplish.

And sometimes, we turn around at the end of it all just to see we've left chaos in our wake, for everyone involved. We intend to be the hero but don't always pay attention to the impact our heroics have on others.

And, like the quintessential super-speed superhero, we're often taken down in our blind spots. Maybe our speed gets the best of us and we leave everyone behind, or we forget to watch out for ourselves amidst it all. We're so busy looking at the dash we're about to make that we miss the bullet coming right for us.

Consider this chapter your post-production slo-mo edit.

We've identified our powers and tracked our heroic journey. Now it's time to break down our super strengths, one step at a time. What you see and do in a proverbial *flash* is what entire teams take years to map out. And the only way to remove the blind spots, protect yourself, and value your strengths is to make your movements visible—first to yourself, then to everyone you're bringing along with you.

We're dropping the bass scale now, so grab your popcorn. This is about to get wicked cool.

AN INHERENT METHOD FOR CHANGE

Certain models of change are universally true and relatively unchanging. The scientific method, design thinking, action learning, lean startup—at their core, every path toward change shares the same basic structure. Sense the system to create a first vision, take a step toward it, then iterate your next steps based on the results the action created.

Hypothesize, experiment, analyze.

Define, ideate, prototype.

Build, measure, learn.

Vision, action, iteration.

In each case, action leads to results, which leads to learning, which informs new action. This is the Catalyst Formula: Vision, Action, Iteration. And we believe it's innate in us.

Within our research, this became evident when Catalysts defined themselves using phrases such as:

"Catalyzing means being clear on the long-term picture—and I'm willing to fail and experiment to bring it to fruition."

"I don't give up."

"I'm happiest when tinkering and experimenting."

"I've learned how important it is to have a learning mindset and to never become complacent."

"I have an idea, but I'm not attached to the specific outcome or how I have to get there."

Yet, we rarely hear Catalysts describe these traits in a way that conveys them in ways that organizations appreciate. They say, "I connect the dots," not, "I do extensive research." To be fair, even when we can describe our value, not everyone will be ready to see it. But simply understanding that our innate process *is* valuable and then learning to articulate it as best we can, is a gamechanger. In this context, awareness becomes our most important tool.

Awareness allows us to see our strengths for what they are and apply them with intentionality to whatever we're manifesting in our lives. Awareness allows us to harness our powers better than we have in the past—it brings unconscious competence into consciousness. Most importantly, it allows us to see our blind spots and begin to work around them.

Whether Catalysts work on something for five minutes or five years, the mechanisms remain the same. How it feels and how quickly that work pulls us down toward burnout will change with scale, but the work itself remains the same: it's a constant, rapid cycling of the Catalyst Formula. The best way to create this awareness is to slow down the cycles long enough to identify what's happening and bring a quality of mindfulness to every stage of the process. Fortunately, that's also how we can bring people along more effectively.

In other words, we have to employ the slo-mo shot in our work processes to understand the depth of what we're able to do in both short and long cycles.

PAUSE WITH TRACEY

Back at Microsoft, we had to teach the people outside of our department how to use design thinking.[6] When I left that world and started coaching, design wasn't part of my everyday life anymore, or so I thought.

It wasn't until I spoke with a Catalyst that the lightbulb clicked back on. She said, "My skillset is to listen to others' thoughts, wants, and desires... then to engage the group by coalition-building and distilling a simple framework that would galvanize people."

She described collecting data, framing the challenge or problem to be solved, co-creating a framework as the output of the data collection, and bringing people together around that framework to orchestrate the change moving forward. As she unintentionally laid out the design thinking process I had a revelation.

Catalysts are often drawn to work that utilizes design thinking, or intrigued when they're introduced to it, because it normalizes their internal processes.

This is a key part of the Catalyst's process—just how frequently and intensely they experience data collection and synthesis—and it's important to understand what that means so we can better support and utilize it in ourselves and the Catalysts around us.

Yet Catalysts don't always refer to this energetic data-synthesis stage as research, but that's what's going on. Another Catalyst that I coached was very matter of fact about it: "At the beginning of any good project, of course I would go and do my research." The beginning phase of seeing

---

6   For a general introduction to design thinking, I recommend Nigel Cross, *Design Thinking: Understanding How Designers Think and Work*. For design thinking within organizations, read Tim Brown, *Change by Design: How Design Thinking Transforms Organizations and Inspires Innovation*.

a change that's going to work is understanding the environment and actors. Why wouldn't it be?

Except that's anything but normal. If you are a Catalyst by nature, you're gathering information and using it to inform your visions and actions similar to a researcher. In fact, when we bring in the internal consultant or hire a big management consulting firm, they're trained in research but might not be able to understand the environment and actors as well as a highly motivated Catalyst can. Your "dot connecting" and "systems thinking" superpowers are research and design thinking by another name—this is the Catalyst Formula naturally happening for you. The challenge we bring you is to begin to recognize and use your natural process with more consciousness and intentionality.

SUPERPOWERS AND BLIND SPOTS

Successful CEOs and highly effective executives often share similar routines and practices that make them successful. They talk about having deep clarity on their ultimate vision. They say they know what they're working toward from the time they wake up in the morning. And they have practices in place that support the action they're inevitably going to take.

These practices stand out to us precisely because they aren't common. Many people within an organization have their head down, doing what's in front of them, hoping to reach a concrete outcome rather than questioning how things could be better and developing their own vision of a better future achieved by more flexible and agile ways of working. Creativity is stifled, and that often leads to stagnant, dormant teams who need to be pulled into a vision and taught how to iterate.

While the Catalyst ultimately holds the same basic habits as those successful CEOs around coming to a vision and driving it toward action, not all of us find ourselves at the executive's table. Even when we are, we're often treated like a virus in the organization rather than the solution. Our rapidly moving vision is perceived as an untreatable threat rather than an opportunity.

This isn't all the fault of the organization for missing our value. We are also susceptible to our own blind spots that keep us from delivering value in a way that the organization can appreciate or even accept.

Each process for change and innovation can be distilled down to three phases—Vision, Action, and Iteration—that loop together until the change is realized. That process, or the Catalyst Formula, is clearly reflected in the way Catalysts identify their inner workings: connect the dots, set it in motion, learn continually.

A Catalyst in motion lives out the Vision, Action, Iteration formula in hyperdrive, and that speed can turn the hero's rescue into a mass of chaos with what seems like the slightest misstep. With some awareness and mindfulness, we can not only approach each piece of the formula with intention but also at a slower pace that our people are more likely to follow.

VISION

Where the larger population crafts a singular vision, often as a set of goals, Catalysts are constantly in visioning-mode. Part of our superpower is the intake of vast amounts of data and the ability to synthesize it quickly. It's like having thousands of tiny tentacles all over the place at once, feeling out potentially relevant information. Perhaps, years from this writing, there will be a measurable field or tracking device that makes this ability tangible. Perhaps it will become a visible skill, and we'll better see and understand why so much data inference can become overstimulating and exhausting.

For now, here's a quick delineation of some categories of data that we're collecting at any given moment:

- **Emotional data:** reading the room, picking up on unspoken needs, getting an intuitive sense that there is a problem or potential solution
- **Literal data:** information, words, charts, statistics, numbers—both presented and sought out
- **Conversational data:** discussions and feedback that help us build and appropriately iterate within our unique context
- **Systemic data:** understanding our organization and the actors within it, including information across organizational siloes
- **Artistic data:** pulling inspiration from the collective (un)consciousness through movies, novels, music, and other creative expressions

Each new piece of information that we take in shapes the Catalyst's vision more and more. We're constantly making it better, in real time, energized by the flow of information. Some Catalysts catch overarching visions for a future state—e.g., "A computer on every desk and in *every* home"—while others are more adept at visioning the *how* and seeing more detailed steps fall into place. Both are equally valid and pose a similar challenge: we may not be aware that we've come to a vision or how to best present it to the world. That's where our blind spots come in.

If anyone is going to play a supporting role in realizing the vision with us, we have to be highly intentional about how and when (and perhaps how many times) we share it with them, or we'll lose them.

The challenge for Catalysts is that a vision for change comes together clearly, almost all on its own, so much so that we don't always realize it's happening. A new, better future state kind of appears to us as we take in information. It comes so naturally, and we see it so clearly that we tend to assume others see it that naturally, too. In fact, saying something about it might feel sophomoric—*of course* everyone else got to the same point. Didn't they?

Coming to a vision happens at a level of unconscious competence, so that we not only forget to mention the a-ha moment to others, but we can also miss it ourselves. New visions supplant previous visions, and we don't even notice things are changing. In fact, we've not only forgotten what version 1.0 vision looked like, we've forgotten that that version ever existed. The new vision that's in front of us is obviously the way to go, so we head off in that direction without thinking twice. We've moved the goal post for success without even realizing it. But our team noticed.

As we constantly move through Vision, Action, and Iteration, we can sometimes sweep people into the process way too early for their comfort levels. When we share too soon, our disruptive ideas can ultimately diminish our influence. *We* know that not all of our ideas are going to stick around until lunchtime—and that's exciting for us. But our teams tend to see that kind of shifting as fickle rather than flexible.

We're not often tied to a specific outcome, but measurable results are still important to most people—especially our teams and bosses. Slowing down to understand and maximize the Catalyst Formula helps us to demonstrate our work more clearly and keep others on board as needed.

ACTION AND ORCHESTRATION

Our most familiar movement as Catalysts is action. As definitive as it sounds, it can be rather nuanced and subtle. We often see Catalysts creating action in a variety of ways that they wouldn't name for themselves.

In fact, as we worked through the material for this chapter, defining action was a challenge at first. In society as a whole, action is assumed to be measurable and concrete, when that's not always the case.

Action is about movement, no matter how subtle it might be. Some Catalysts are excellent at bringing all of the moving parts together and implementing the vision they set out with. Others simply move forward, learning and adapting as they go, whether or not they see the final iteration play out. For all Catalysts, however, action at a fundamental level is simply stepping out from the hypothesis and beginning to test.

When the Catalyst Formula moves at catalytic speed, action steps are often blurred. Data is our energizer, and both vision and iteration are centered around it. Yet, the action we take to create more data and move toward the vision is worth identifying, naming, and amplifying, because action is valued as a measurable, tangible thing in an organization. If we can identify the kinds of actions we're skilled at, we can offer those skills up as something an organization or a team might better track as a metric, return, or result. This isn't an easy process, which is why we have an entire chapter on tools for it in part 2.

No matter the scope, impact, or metrics of the actions we take, the bottom line for Catalysts is that we thrive when we're moving forward, making things happen, and ultimately bringing a vision closer to manifestation. The ultimate purpose of each action will shift from person to person and within different scenarios, and so will the outcome. This is a frequent point of contention for newly identifying Catalysts—how much action "counts?"

"If I have seven potential things to action on and five have stalled out, am I really a Catalyst?"

"If I'm making things better quietly and behind the scenes, without anyone knowing that I've taken action, does it still count?"

First of all, only you can know whether the label of Catalyst helps you work well. But let us take some of the weight off of it for you: we all have things that keep us from taking action. We might be held back by a lack of confidence or imposter syndrome. We might hold back when we lack clarity, or when a clear vision seems too big and overwhelming to tackle.

Often, taking one step toward a vision is enough to jumpstart confidence and bring in more data to create clarity.

A Catalyst's action can look like any of the following:

- Getting feedback on your vision from key stakeholders and trusted sources
- Updating your vision after gathering feedback
- Co-creation, including bringing both resistors and supporters together to identify action steps
- Small steps, like putting a meeting on the calendar or writing one blog post
- Big steps, like shipping a product or publishing a book (the small steps are what lead to the big steps)

When action is stalled at any point, we tend to suffer, because the drive toward change is part of our nature. Without action, we lose our pathway to more feedback. We lose our ability to build confidence and create clarity. And especially when action stalls as a result of resistance, we often believe it's because of who we are and can begin to drop down that slippery slope toward burnout.

The bottom line is that we are *going* to move into action. It's definitional to us as Catalysts, even if your action doesn't look the same as someone else's. The less intentional we are in that step, however, the less likely we'll be to orchestrate action effectively.

Step back into that place of empathy for a moment and consider what it's like for the people around us when we step into action. We're assuming the vision is clear to everyone, but we might not have shared it with the right people at the right time.

We're dumping that manic energy into movement that they might not be ready to receive. We're shifting as the feedback comes in and the next action needs to be different. And then we wonder why we can't keep our teams and bosses on board.

Embracing this side of ourselves enables us to slow it down enough to bring our people along with us, and that ultimately serves the larger change.

ITERATION

Learning, mistakes, and failures are part of the natural path that any innovator will take, and that's especially true for Catalysts. Often, organizations put constraints such as SMART goals on us, especially when we're pursuing an amorphous (to them) goal or are swimming outside of our lane. *Specific, Measurable, Achievable, Relevant, and Time-Bound* restrictions quantify the delivery and are useful to measure most paths of innovation.

But for the Catalyst who is not only open to failure but welcoming it as part of their process, the constraints can feel forced and limiting. For us, the measurement of forward progress is not energizing or useful if it neglects to pivot in response to current information.

As action brings in new data, Catalysts apply that feedback to the vision. Restrictive goals make us feel bound to outdated plans and objectives. Our goal is not to make things but to make things *better*. We're not going to keep moving forward into a vision that becomes obsolete based on feedback.

This isn't to say we can't work within the system we're given, but understanding our iterative process can begin to explain why we chafe under these kinds of goals—and can potentially point to resistance or other issues that lead an organization to leash us to those constraints in the first place.

When we're able to iterate freely within our formula, both results *and* resistance provide feedback that inform the next action and the ultimate execution of the vision we set out to realize. When we tackle personal issues in this way, our speed of iteration carries little consequence. You can shift your vision for how you want to lose weight, write more, or spend your free time as much as you'd like without affecting anyone else. As soon as we need to bring others on board, however, the story changes.

Even though we typically pivot based on reliable data, we don't always share that data in a way that others can appreciate and follow. Sometimes, we don't share at all. If we don't provide enough updated information for our teams to keep up with, our cyclones of energy turn into a trap for our people.

This is especially problematic when we don't bring it to our own consciousness because iteration and action function as a self-contained production line for the drug that is problem-solving mania. Our speed of iteration creates a sense of quicksand for our teams, who then resist, which tells us to iterate around that resistance, which pulls us down, which tells us to go back to what feeds us...Without intentionality and mindfulness, the mania drug of problem-solving can quickly become a poison.

Unconscious iteration is a superpower, to be sure, but it's one that we can amplify by slowing down to reflect more intentionally.

As we learn how to pause for the sake of others and for the sake of the process, we can also learn how to pause for our own sake as well. The more mindfulness we have in the process, the more likely we'll be to differentiate positive iteration from the iteration spiral into burnout that we're so prone to.

And once we've done that, moments of failure are nothing more than feedback. The more we have developed a foundation of self-compassion along with a healthy separation between ourselves and our work, the more able we are to see the "failure" for what it is: the opportunity to inject more information into our formula.

THE CONTAINER OF REJUVENATION

There is a story that we tell ourselves about rejuvenation, or our collective lack thereof. We tell ourselves that the mission is more important than we are. The only way to achieve the mission is through self-sacrifice, so we don't think about the personal cost. In reality, a constantly burned out changemaker isn't helping anyone at all.

Without seeing this process on a microscopic scale or slowing it down to half-speed, we bundle up our work as simply part of who we are. Our ideas are ours. We're driven by passion that's ours. In the best of times, we're given credit for the magic, too. So when we're blocked from taking action, are met with resistance, or lose people along the way, we tend to internalize that as ours as well. In the last chapter, we saw just how quickly that lack of distance can pull us down into burnout.

To be fair, sometimes it is on us. There are skills we can learn and tools we can employ in order to lessen the impacts of rapid change on people around us. But even when we do everything right, change is never easy. It's still going to be difficult for our teammates, peers, and bosses. We're still going to run into resistance, and we're still going to run ourselves into the ground. Without some separation between who we are and what we do, even the best of circumstances can wear us down.

We've found that Catalysts function at their highest when their changemaking is kept in a container—specifically, the container of a rejuvenation practice.

Rejuvenation allows us to self-regulate through the various stages of the energy curve so that we can be more intentional in our responses. It allows us to vision better, get more clarity, operate more efficiently, and bring other people along. It helps us tap into empathy for others and compassion for ourselves. It allows us to sustain our energy and deepen our resilience when things get tough—and they will get tough.

By replacing self-sacrifice with self-awareness, compassion, and self-care, we create spaciousness between ourselves and the work. Imagine cramming you, your colleagues, your boss, your relationships, your hobbies, and your drive for change all inside a giant balloon. Now imagine what that balloon would feel like being pulled from the top. That tension removes all of the space that we need to move. Pulled tight enough, eventually it feels like we're going to snap. And we might.

Often, we're not able to step back and articulate what's happening or pause long enough to orchestrate because our world is a balloon that's about to pop.

Embedding rejuvenation practices within each step of the formula helps make the world—and our capacity for change—bigger.

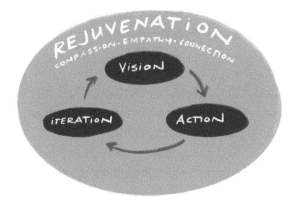

Rejuvenation does slow us down a bit, but the pause creates room for a more mindful approach to work that has a higher likelihood of success. Mindfully choosing rejuvenation as a way to support your natural catalytic process is key to minimizing the frequency and depth of burnout.

The pause helps to minimize workplace trauma on all sides, keeping us from burning out as hard as we would otherwise. In the end, it actually makes us faster, spending fewer cycles iterating and less time bringing others along, and increasing our chances of success.

Rejuvenation acknowledges the fact that our minds *and* our bodies are both part of this process of changemaking. They are our vehicles for change in the world. Without mental, physical, and emotional care, they will break down, taking our innovative ability down with them.

MINDFULNESS AND THE CATALYST FORMULA

We have found it impossible to help Catalysts through their journey and within their formula without a heavy focus on rejuvenation. This will be evident throughout part 2 of the book, as each tool has its own rejuvenation component on top of the whole-self rejuvenating practices that need their own focus.

There is a great deal of flex in what those practices actually look like—what rejuvenates Tracey won't necessarily be the same for Shannon or for you. As we discussed last chapter, we've found that the major categories come down to consistent routines, self-compassion, community, and empathy for others. Whatever enables these practices in your life will rejuvenate you and enable a better, more effective workflow and outcome.

Overlaying them all, however, is a sense of mindfulness and intentionality that must start early on in a new challenge.

More and more, scientific research is exploring all of the benefits of mindfulness and meditation, especially in the workplace. Specifically for Catalysts, mindfulness supports us and our work in a way that little else can. It is how we bring the Catalyst Formula forward into consciousness, how we contain it with consistent rejuvenation, and how we recover when burnout takes us down.

HOW MINDFULNESS KEEPS US MOVING: MEG LEVIE

Mindfulness—slowing down enough to see what's happening and become more intentional in our steps—is a key way to cultivate a deeper sense of self-awareness, which is a foundational tool in becoming our most successful Catalyst selves. But while it's easy enough to see what mindfulness can *do*, it's important to key in on what mindfulness actually *is*.

Recently, we spoke with Meg Levie, a trained Zen Priest, Mindfulness Executive Coach, and early co-creator of the Search Inside Yourself Leadership Institute (SIYLI). Meg describes mindfulness as "simply being aware" or "being aware of self, others, and the environment with an attitude of curiosity and kindness." She continues, "It's not about making everything perfect and having some ideal condition to be mindful, it's really being present and aware of whatever is happening."

In other words, mindfulness is an invitation for us to allow our minds to be fully present in what we are doing in the moment.[7] From there, we can develop both clarity about the moment and about ourselves. To use an old Zen proverb: "When walking, walk. When eating, eat."

Being mindful and present provides a sense of freedom and a spaciousness that allows us to be non-reactive. It helps us cultivate curiosity for ourselves, our thoughts, our surroundings, our situation, and those around us. This allows us to develop new awareness and insights. Practicing mindfulness within the Catalyst Formula holds us higher on the energy curve throughout our journey, simply by creating spaciousness and distance between ourselves and our work.

---

7   In *Wherever You Go, There You Are*, Jon Kabat-Zinn, a pioneer in the Mindfulness movement, says that "Mindfulness means paying attention in a particular way: on purpose, in the present moment, and nonjudgmentally."

As a starting point, mindfulness meditation is a particularly powerful self-awareness tool that has been used for thousands of years and is an excellent supportive practice for your experience engaging with the concepts and tools in this book. Where mindfulness is a state of being, meditation is the activity we do to cultivate mindfulness.

Some other simple ways to cultivate mindfulness include bringing awareness to everyday activities, journaling, gratitude practices, asking for routine feedback from friends or co-workers, yoga, or working with a coach or mentor. Not only is that just a small starting point, but you can further explore and create your own practices by combining several activities until you find what suits you.

If mindfulness is like strength, meditation is like lifting weights. And like any exercise, there are many forms of meditation, with different types of focus and forms to support the practice. There are informal practices and formal practices. Most major religions of the world have some form of meditation, and there are a variety of drivers for people to meditate— for clarity, wisdom, enlightenment, transformation, non-reactivity, stress reduction, self-compassion, and loving kindness. There's really no "right" or "wrong" way to approach meditation—simply showing up as you are is an act of presence and mindfulness in itself.

For many meditation practices, and many of those we bring into our work with Catalysts, the focus is on cultivating the mindfulness that practitioners like Meg and pioneers like Jon Kabat-Zinn describe to deepen our sense of self-awareness, with no "goal" other than letting our mind learn to experience this very moment and ourselves without judgement or attachment. We notice when our mind wanders. And when it does, because that's what brains do, we gently and non-judgmentally notice where it floats off to, and perhaps the emotions underneath those thoughts. Then we return our attention to the present moment.

Witnessing ourselves and our thoughts is a deeply effective way to develop self-awareness. This also softens our sense of self to help us see it as more fluid and relational rather than rigid and unchanging.

Meg explains that Catalysts without that relational sense of self may have a hard time on a typical Catalyst journey where they quickly and repeatedly go from being loved to be vilified. "You may feel like you're on the rollercoaster. You're holding onto that car and it goes up and you're like, 'Wow! Great! I'm so great! Everybody loves me!' But then you just know the roller coaster is going to go down. And if you're holding onto it tightly, you're going to go down, too, thinking 'Oh no, everyone hates me. I'm awful.'"

Self-awareness and mindfulness give you the equanimity (the mental calmness and composure) to respond to the roller coaster differently. "Mindfulness means opening to and remembering deep truths of imper-manence and interconnectedness as we go about our daily life, and acting in accordance with our values" You can feel the joy and the pain in each moment, but you realize that you're bigger than either of them. Those feelings stem from a co-created event that you were just a part of, which doesn't define you.

Mindfulness and self-awareness can help you re-contextualize when-ever it feels appropriate. You may try asking yourself, "Am I stuck in this narrative? Is it serving me now?"

Self-awareness serves as a foundation for many of the skills we can develop to make us more effective Catalysts: self-compassion, empathy, and setting a more deliberate pace. Each of these skills stems from self-awareness and will be supported by a regular mindfulness practice, however that takes shape for you.

YOUR UNIQUE PROCESS

Like any formula, there will be variables that change the shape of the Catalyst Formula. From the pieces of the process that we naturally love, to the aspects that are especially challenging for our organizations, each of us has our own strengths and struggles to leverage or overcome. That's why we are tracking patterns and connections in Catalysts, not creating templates. It's also why we have spent so much time on self-awareness in this section.

The context of your role or organization will create its own needs, pitfalls, and blind spots. So will your personality, values, and purpose in life. To try to pigeonhole you to one type of change, one kind of manifestation, one level of execution would be to strip you of your powers. That's why we aren't working on the process of change here. We're working on the self-actualization of the change*maker*.

As long as your Catalyst tendencies are subconscious, it's difficult to identify a clear, replicating pattern in the way that you work. Without a clear pattern, it's difficult to know when there is a break that needs to be repaired. From another angle: the ability to name and optimize the way that you work allows you to leverage those abilities now and in the future.

If we struggle to bring parts of this process to consciousness, it's likely the same reason our bosses miss it as well: because we're all conditioned to look for outputs. We conflate execution with action and do whatever is necessary to get a new vision to that stage. But if we can literally slow down time to watch ourselves work, we would see just how much we're accomplishing at every step. People don't hire us because we're magical. They hire us because we get shit done, and the tools to follow can help us do that much more efficiently.

We're not telling you to change what you're doing at all. We're simply going to optimize what's already innate within you. To create the container of rejuvenation that houses incredible change. To allow you to see yourself in slow-motion, making epic things happen all around you. To take the time to build out a cohesive vision, orchestrate through action as much as necessary, iterate with others in mind, and never forget that your mind and body are worth protecting, even if you only think of them as a vehicle for the change you want to see in the world.

The next time the bass scale drops, you'll be ready. And we can't wait to see what you'll leave in your wake.

THRIVING WITHIN THE CATALYST FORMULA

☐ **Our natural process.** Catalysts have an unconscious process they use to drive change that includes Vision, Action, and Iteration that we call the Catalyst Formula.

☐ **Make it conscious.** Making the Catalyst Formula conscious can make us more effective at driving change and minimizing burnout.

☐ **Mindfulness is key.** We can most clearly see the Catalyst Formula in action when we're practicing mindfulness to bring those steps to awareness.

☐ **Consistent rejuvenation is the antidote.** When we don't wrap the Formula in consistent rejuvenation marked by self-compassion, empathy, and community, burnout happens frequently and with great intensity.

☐ **Clarify and connect.** Every offering that we provide for Catalysts is centered around clarifying the Catalyst Formula and being more effective within it so that you can thrive. For more clarity on the process and connection to a larger community of Catalysts doing the same work, visit www.CatalystConstellations.com.

PART II

THE CATALYST SUPPORTED

CHAPTER 4

ENABLING VISION

At twenty-five years old, Michael was the VP of Finance for the company he started with as an intern. He lived in a beautiful spot in southern California, was in a relationship with a beautiful girl, and was driving his dream (yes, beautiful) car. By all external indicators, he had it all. But Michael is a Catalyst, and Catalysts rarely "arrive."

It took a few years of discontent and searching for a new thing to catalyze. Michael likes to quote Albert Einstein here, saying, "If I had sixty minutes to solve a problem, I would spend fifty-five minutes thinking of the right question to ask." Michael sat with the problem of purpose while continuing to work in finance, and with his catalytic data collection powers at full speed, he spotted an opportunity that had been close to him from the beginning.

Looking back over the years at his company, he noticed several real estate moves that they'd made in connection with cell phone towers. Private owners who had rooftop space and unused parking lots were renting them out for cell phone towers at $1,000 a month, and his company was offering $100,000 to buy it up from those owners as an example. Never mind what his company was doing with the property—that was two separate paydays for landowners who had otherwise completely unused property. That, Michael realized, was exactly the kind of thing he wanted to manifest next.

If he could invest in a way that earned something like those lottery-ticket double payouts he'd seen happen earlier in his career, that kind of financial freedom could support almost any catalytic vision he could spin up in the future. So he did.

Michael went from absolutely no real estate holdings, to a total of $4 million in cash flowing commercial real estate, by the time he bought his first home (opposite of most people). He's been growing his real estate business ever since.

This time around, he knew that the payday alone wasn't what he wanted. There had to be a deeper purpose, or he would be left in the same position all over again, having checked all the boxes but not satisfying that deeper need for meaning and relevance in the world. Today, Michael is involved in several projects that are energizing and meaningful to him, including a massive space station that's eighty times bigger than anything else being considered.

Can we repeat that for emphasis? He's developing a massive *space station.*

"I realized there was something still inside of me, burning, so I identified a way to support it. As a Catalyst, I didn't have to know what *it* was going to be. I just needed to utilize the resources around me, and that gave me the time, money, and freedom that I would need." The early concept of the space station was percolating when he attended one of our retreats. Meeting a Catalyst at the retreat who worked at NASA really fanned the flame.

"As a Catalyst, constantly blazing some trail which can sometimes burn you, it is extremely important to have your support system, and no one is a better supporter than a fellow Catalyst."

As we see over and over, having other Catalysts around you can not only help you refine your vision, but their connections can help us see bigger visions, and their belief in our ability to achieve them ignites the fire to create great wicked-big, bold solutions.

Michael wasn't always a big-thinking Catalyst. But starting in high school, Michael has moved quickly from one vision to the next. He recalls a pivotal moment at sixteen years old and newly licensed to drive, when his car was sideswiped in a tragic accident. Michael had no injuries at all, not even scratches from climbing out over broken glass—but two friends sustained injuries and one lost his life.

"After that, nothing tasted the same, nothing smelled the same, nothing felt the same. I didn't know what it meant, but I made a decision to make something of the opportunity I'd been given to live."

It took time for him to identify exactly what that purpose was, but he started looking for it right away. He graduated early, pivoted away from college quickly, succeeded in finance, then moved on to real estate, and now that has lost its luster in the face of facilitating space exploration. The lessons he learns or accomplishments he reaches in each previous manifestation tend to drive the next. High school to college is an obvious one, but finance to real estate is less so. Real estate to space station is something only a Catalyst can do.

As one vision is realized and another comes into view, Michael notes that burnout tends to set in. "When I accomplish those things, I'm good. It just fizzles out." That doesn't mean he gets to quit. Burnout in one thing often coincides with energy in another. "Last year was a tough year," he says of real estate, "but at the same time, the space station project was giving me so much life. It has been amazing—it's why I'm here."

All along his journey, Michael has grown closer and closer to his sense of intuition. If something didn't feel right—like finishing high school on a normal pace, or staying in college at all, or coasting along with his early success—he paid attention to those signals and made a change. He started preparing for it and making space in his finances and lifestyle. The drive was so clear and strong, in fact, that he believes the search for meaning is what makes us Catalysts in the first place.

The more self-aware he became, the more remarkable his life became in response.

Michael warns Catalysts that it's easy to focus on the vision, but we tend to forget the pragmatic steps needed to make that vision come to life—including the finances to make it possible and people we need to help us along the way.

He leverages his superpower, the ability to articulate his vision with the wins in mind to gain support from potential allies. This has served him well while creating bigger, bolder visions. As he engages some of the world's top scientists, government officials and investors he approaches them with absolute clarity of what the win will be for them.

It's a simple focus but one that holds true: we need each other in this world. And, apparently, on other worlds, too.

SUPERPOWERS AND BLIND SPOTS

When a Catalyst first starts a job or a project, we tend to see wicked problems that are like dragons that we're destined to slay, and all we can think about is the problem. Like Michael experienced, it's consuming enough to energize us even as we sink into burnout from other things—and even though that hyperfocus on the problem can eventually tip us back toward burnout in the end. In the meantime, we see data everywhere we look, in every conversation we have, and our energy builds as we know the answer is just around the corner.

Once the vision snaps into place, we see the potential future so clearly that we can't help but move toward it. The problem is that we tend to see what others don't. We're following the dots that we connected to make a path toward something better, while people around us might not even see the dots at all. Because we're moving so quickly, we rarely pause to make the vision clear. We might even forget to say it out loud.

UNCERTAIN FUTURE   CATALYST'S CERTAIN
                              FUTURE

To enhance our superpowers and open up our blind spots, we need to expand spaciousness and creativity as well as zoom back into a strategic sense of focus.

Our ability to see a better future is a skill that few leaders are lucky to possess. In his book *Double Double*, Cameron Herold trademarked his "Vivid Vision" process as a way for productivity-focused businesspeople to begin to create this spaciousness for themselves and their teams specifically for the purpose of visioning.

The Vivid Vision process is centered around turning off screens, stepping out into nature, thinking broadly about your objectives, and writing them down with a pen and paper. He asks his readers to answer future-minded questions that Catalysts often process instinctively, if not subconsciously:

- How will people talk about your business after this is done?
- How will the organization talk about it?
- What are customers going to say?

By physically moving into a new space and utilizing your mental space in a different way, he posits that anyone can move into this future space and come to a clearer vision.

...and all the Catalysts said, "Wasn't *everyone* doing that?"

At the very least, we would do that if we could carve out the time. For someone who already finds themselves making connections in the shower or jotting down ideas or getting up from their desk to take a walk and think, it can be interesting to hear these things taught as groundbreaking tactics. We often take informal learning journeys to bring the pieces together, and the vision becomes a synthesis of this ongoing process of data collection. We hear what other stakeholders are saying, see the problems arising, remember past lessons learned, and eventually come to clear, vivid visions without any formal process at all.

So imagine how much more clarity we'd get if we created space and intention around them.

Imagine how much more buy-in and value we'd create with people around us if we relied on active listening at all stages.

Imagine how much bigger the vision could be if it were built out of collective experience, wisdom, and value.

PAUSE WITH SHANNON

In my role at Vodafone, I had the amazing opportunity to design and run over one hundred Innovation Workshops with C-Level executives from the world's largest companies and organizations (like Unilever, United Nations, Coca-Cola, Citibank, Hitachi, CARE, General Electric). As you can imagine, the ability to vision new futures is the essence of an Innovation Workshop. Creating both the templates and structures for the Innovation Workshops was a dream job—finally, I had found a job that fit my Catalyst self. Using my dot-connecting superpowers to sense the latest emerging trends to share across the organization and with customer executives allowed me to tap into that euphoric feeling people describe when you are *in flow*.

Even before landing this dream job, I had readily embraced Design Thinking as something that described how my brain worked. For years, I had been spending time with customers, trying to understand their business, watching how they used technology and iterating in ways that made solutions more meaningful to them. Applying this as a foundation to the innovation process just made sense. At the same time, my innate experimentation mindset meant that I was not married to one perspective and was constantly looking for ways to enhance and iterate our practices to produce the best outcomes. For example, after reading *Lean Startup* by Eric Reis, I sent the book to the entire Innovation Champion team and updated the innovation process flow to include the practice of "build, measure, learn."

With so many data points about what worked and what didn't from so many workshops around the globe, I had the opportunity to Vision, Act, and Iterate on the process of innovation itself.

But it was when I read *Theory U* by Otto Scharmer that I finally found a framing, which described what I had been trying to cultivate in our innovation methodology—a much deeper place of co-creation to develop more purposeful visions of the future. *Theory U* outlines the importance of the quality of consciousness in the innovation process. By suspending our habitual way of thinking, seeing with fresh eyes, and letting go of ego, we can more clearly see what needs to emerge.

From there, as the vision crystalizes, *Theory U* explains the importance of co-creating and prototyping to create systemic change. *Theory U* stresses the importance of the interior condition of the participant, articulating what I had witnessed when workshops were carefully and intentionally orchestrated. It helped me communicate what I had been striving to articulate. It amplified my interest in creating environments where business leaders could have the space and conditions to tap into deeper systemic solutions and allowed me to refine the process even more.[8]

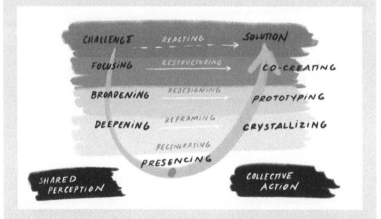

With this view in mind, I organized a three-day co-creation workshop in 2015 in Johannesburg, South Africa, for Vodafone and Novartis. The two companies had previously collaborated to create an amazing program called SMS for Life in 2009—using basic text messaging technology to

---

8   This is a very brief synopsis, and I strongly encourage all Catalysts to explore *Theory U*.

reduce malaria drug stock outages across Africa. It had been a success-ful program and both companies were interested in exploring SMS for Life 2.0, as well as other new potential opportunities.

We started by having the participants explore Novartis' manufacturing and distribution sites, a rural clinic and an urban clinic. Some of these executives had never been on the ground in Africa to see the business firsthand. Additionally, by having leaders from multiple disciplines—both pharma business experts and mobile technology experts—the group was able to explore and ask questions through new lenses. Both teams were able to let go of preconceptions, see what was really going on in the field and sense what needed to emerge. Experiencing and witnessing the "on the ground" realities materially changes the interior condition of the participants. It's no longer theoretical processes and profits; it's real employees, real doctors, and real patients whose lives are being impacted.

Just getting the executives into the field wasn't enough, though. If we had taken them on that amazing Learning Journey and then brought them into a fluorescent lit hotel conference room, the group's ability to think creatively certainly wouldn't have flourished. That interior condition that we so carefully shifted by getting execs into the field would have changed back into "same old" thinking.

We started each Innovation Workshop with a fantastic dinner the night before—allowing participants to relax, get to know each other as indi-viduals, share personal passions, and start to develop trust. In fact, the inception of many of the innovation outputs throughout my time at Voda-fone started at these kickoff dinners when two passionate people sat next to each other. For the workshop itself, we leveraged the new award-winning "green" certified Vodafone Innovation Centre, which focused on beauty and bringing nature into the architectural experience. Allowing people to relax and be inspired by their surroundings has a material impact on the ability to deepen creative systems thinking. Nature has a strong positive impact on the quality of our consciousness.

Though we had laid out all the right pre-conditions for co-creating a new transformational concept, it's not easy getting a large group of people to be able to not only develop their own vision but share it with others, and then have others build on it. To help this process, we brought in a graphic recorder.

Professional visual notetaking is a great supportive tool when you have too many people to draw their own visions or when it may just be too uncomfortable for them. Experiencing art enhances people's creative abilities while providing a common visual language that participants can respond to. "No, that's not what I meant." "Yes! That's exactly how I imagined it." Plus, at the end there's a very clear visual record of what the group agreed to pursue. "Here are the five ideas we're going to prototype." It allowed the group to take the visual artifact back into each organization to cultivate wider understanding, adoption, and momentum.

From this workshop, in 2016, Novartis launched SMS for Life 2.0—expanding the tracking of stock outs to HIV, TB, vaccine, and leprosy treatments, combined with tracking diseases and health outcomes along with e-learning modules for health care workers. The program is still running across Africa—in South Africa, Zambia, Nigeria, Tanzania, and Kenya.

TOOLS TO ENABLE SUCCESS

Company cultures tend to reward strategic deliverables like PowerPoint decks, timelines, and pitches more than atypical practices that create space for creativity. But vision done well—in the way that Catalysts are naturally inclined to—rests at the intersection of both creativity *and* strategy.

Creativity speaks to the need for spaciousness. Just as daydreaming happens within moments of stillness and boredom, creative visioning is facilitated by space for inspiration—whether that's the physical space of nature or the mental space of conversation, art, and open possibilities. But strategy separates vision from daydreaming. It is how we take the data we collected and the future we imagined and connect them to the real-life variables we're working within.

The combination of strategy and creativity is amplified when we co-create in concert with other people—ideas build, swirl, change, and grow when multiple points of view come together.

Tools that hold us at the intersection of creativity and strategy will help us create clearer visions and place them into their relevant context and ultimately serve our need to orchestrate action with the people around us.

PRACTICE ACTIVE LISTENING

As Catalysts, we're often seen as the big ideas person, and we wear it proudly. We can play into the myth that we are given a "gift" of vision. And that's not entirely wrong. But if we're honest about the process—or better yet, if we want to be more intentional about the process to have better outcomes—we need to practice active listening.

So much of the Catalyst's life is spent entering new environments, after being invited in to create change or inviting ourselves in when we just can't help but see how things could be better. Either way, there is no reason to take off and run with *our* vision without first obtaining the proper situational context.

We can expedite the development of a meaningful vision and get people bought-in by practicing a lot of active listening. This means going into a conversation with one primary objective—truly trying to understand the complete message the other party has to say. The point is not to agree with them or try to convince them of your point of view but to actually deeply listen to them.

Active listening looks like showing up with genuine curiosity to understand another's experience or viewpoint. It looks like asking a question and then...just being quiet. Shutting up and *really* listening.

It means using mindfulness to stay present and not spending the time while the other person is talking to think about the next thing you're going to say. It feels like holding long (what might feel like awkward) silence, which actually invites the other person to continue.

Often, people have their own top-level "talk track" running when someone is speaking, playing the story or viewpoint they have shared a hundred times instead of actually hearing what's being said. When they get past that narrative—when the silence or the next gentle question stemming from curiosity, "Tell me more about that," invites them to continue—they can start to hear the real emotions, thoughts, motivations, doubts, or fears underneath the polished stories. And people are so rarely listened to with this type of intention, feeling heard not only uncovers "hidden" truths, but it starts to build a sense of connection and trust as well. Especially when you can take what you heard from them and incorporate their well-being into your vision.

Within new contexts—which we will almost always find ourselves in—we will always run the risk of creating a vision that's right for *our* past experience but not for that organization at that time. When we are truly in service of the best possible future for all parties involved, listening is the best access point for the data we're craving and the dots we want to connect to come to a solution.

SAY THE VISION OUT LOUD

Catalysts frequently say their superpower is connecting the dots and seeing the path forward. Very few say their superpower is *articulating* that opportunity. We synthesize data so much differently from our counterparts that it's not uncommon to hear some version of a complaint that, "We were all in the same meeting together. I don't understand why anyone could be confused about the next steps." The data seems so clear that it doesn't occur to us to clarify it.

To turn clear articulation of the vision into a superpower, start by simply putting that new end state into words. Not a slide-ready version of it—just a simple articulation.

Pause long enough to identify that you've come to a vision, and verbalize what it might look and feel like. This allows us to document a starting point, choose a potential end point, and create a focal point for our energy—and those things are absolutely vital for any kind of collaboration. By speaking your vision as a manifesto of sorts, it forces a pause and brings the vision into better focus.

When we first started talking about Catalyst Constellations, our vision statement was simply that, "We have to help people

who are like us feel like they're supported and not crazy."
That's it. We gave ourselves room to grow and develop and
iterate—and we still have that room to this day.

TAP INTO CREATIVITY

Once a vision has been verbalized as a vision statement, it's
impossible to stop thinking about it. It's percolating while
we work, eat, sleep, and play—if we manage to do any of
those things at all. Engaging your brain in creative thinking
inevitably leads to new connections—both literally as neural
connections and figuratively as new ways for the vision to
snap into place.

According to Kampylis and Berki, "Creative thinking is
defined as the thinking that enables students to apply their
imagination to generating ideas, questions, and hypotheses,
experimenting with alternatives and evaluating their own
and their peers' ideas, final products, and processes."[9]

Imagining *any* challenge and ways we might overcome it
makes us more flexible and ready for any *other* challenge.[10]
Just be careful not to turn on your performance centers by
setting artistic standards for yourself. Not everyone feels
inclined toward creativity, and it's easy to miss the power
of an exercise like drawing or using modeling clay if you're
trying to create a masterpiece. Here are some entry points
that we've used to cut through the mental noise and make
space for creativity:

---

9   Panagiotis Kampylis and Eleni Berki, *Nurturing Creative Thinking* (France: Gonnet Imprimeur, 2014), 6,
    http://unesdoc.unesco.org/images/0022/002276/227680e.pdf.

10 In *The Power of Habit*, Charles Duhigg digs further into this remarkable concept.

- Let's close our eyes for a moment and create some mental space for what we need to do here today.
- For just a few minutes, let's get quiet and each draw an image of what we think we're all working toward.
- There's some tactile clay in front of each of you—let's spend a little bit of time having fun envisioning our work in a different way. Build a quick model of what you'd like to see us work toward.

However you express it, creativity helps us tap into the dreams and creative side, which is essential when we are solving problems that have never been solved before.

CREATE AN ACTION MAP

Once you have a vision of the future state, begin to envision what it might take to get there. Tackle it from angles you hadn't thought of initially. And yes, if you're tracking with us, this is technically an action that will create feedback for iteration on the vision itself. Vision, Action, and Iteration repeat frequently at every stage, and this is no exception. In fact, that's why we need an Action Map: to track your intended path so that the whirlwind of iteration doesn't take you away from it.

To create your map, begin with your starting point and envisioned future state, something like the image we've included here.

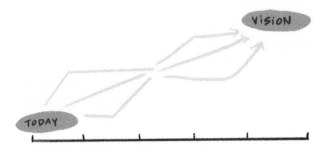

If you're comfortable doing so, give that future an imagined date. Making the map finite makes it more concrete and purposeful, even if you're fully aware that the date is going to change.

Now, note some of the steps that you might need to take along the way. What do you imagine will need to happen to take you from point A to point B? You might draw this as a winding path or a linear line, and you wouldn't be wrong either way. We're drawing the Action Map so that we can see a path that will begin to direct our action, and so that we have a reference point to return to and iterate as those first action steps help us make the next ones more effective.

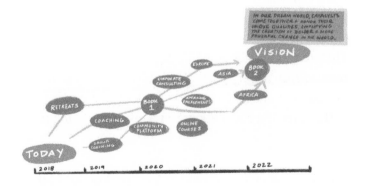

MAKE A NOT RIGHT NOW LIST

Your Action Map can start with everything that might be relevant to the vision, but be sure to whittle it down to what's actually necessary. We are prone to hold onto all of the ideas that we spawn, even when they aren't in direct service of the larger goal (or sustaining ourselves through that work). Then, when we move through a day without making progress on each and every one of those ideas, we judge ourselves for not doing enough.

We call these spawned ideas *phantom goals*, and they don't have a place on your Action Map or your conscience.

Phantom goals are all of those extra ideas that we'd like to accomplish but won't move the larger vision forward. The problem isn't the ideas—it's that we unconsciously hold ourselves to them even when we aren't consciously focused on them (and shouldn't be).

Instead, identify and set aside those phantom goals that are separate from the actual vision you're mapping. This is your Not Right Now list. Those ideas don't have to go away forever, but the Action Map is about this specific envisioned future. If it doesn't get you there, it doesn't belong on *this* map.

The great thing about a Not Right Now list is that there's room to spawn every phantom idea-baby into goals that could one day become real. It's a place to honor those idea babies without feeling badly about not actively pursuing them at this moment.

With that said, *you* do belong on your own Action Map.

Seeing yourself, or the health of your team, as part of the path to action helps us to make more realistic plans that we can actually carry out. Since rejuvenation is the container for all of the work that we do, consider what you'll need to be able to sustain that work from beginning to end, and make sure you give those things a space on the Action Map. Having a map to refer to allows you to say yes to the right things and no to the superfluous things—phantom goals included—that pull us away from the vision we really want to bring into the world.

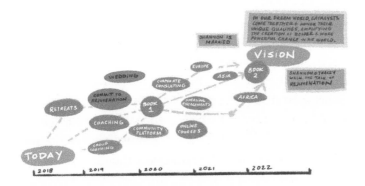

DON'T SHARE TOO SOON

To this point, all of the tools we've highlighted can be done alone or within a tight circle of trusted people. But eventually, the vision will need a test drive. If we share a nascent idea with someone who's naturally critical, we'll drive right into a wall. It kills our confidence and we shelve the idea. That doesn't mean we don't need feedback or to be challenged—we just need to understand when and where those challenges are helpful.

A gentleman named Edward DeBono published a book in the '80s called *Six Thinking Hats*. One of the thinking hats was the black hat, and it represented a line of questioning that was meant to find flaws. Those questions help us see the risks and potential failure, and make the vision stronger and more resilient. But they aren't helpful if they happen too early.

Seeking input and sharing the idea too early creates problems for others, too. Every new idea that's shared prematurely sends out unintentional but very real waves of uncertainty and fear. If we announce everything that we're seeing in that early storming phase to people who are under our charge, it can limit our ability to orchestrate action with them later on.

Carefully choose someone you can talk to, such as a peer outside of your team or organization, who can hear your vision or help you shape your Action Map, but who won't feel threatened by it. It should also be someone who can challenge you without *you* feeling threatened. Bounce it off of them first, allowing them to help you refine your thoughts and translate the vision for the appropriate audiences before you take it to the people it will affect.

OPEN UP TO CHALLENGES

When we create an updated vision for Catalyst Constellations, we work on it together, growing and expanding it from our combined understanding. But we don't stop there. Next, we have a couple of trusted people who we feel safe sharing a fresh idea with. They're able to give us feedback on what we missed, what won't work, and where we need to rethink details.

Because we have already worked through the vision to an extent, and because we trust those select people to challenge the idea without criticizing *us*, we're able to push and expand and tighten and hone it without being crushed in the process. By the time we have shaped it into something solid and our trusted people have poked and prodded it, the idea will have legs to stand on once the critics appear.

In the early stages of an idea like this, you might use questions like these to begin to think bigger and refine the vision:

- What do you know about what you are building, growing, manifesting, and moving toward?
- Once you have reached this "destination," what will it be like? What are attributes of that state/destination?
- Is there anyone there with you?
- What will it feel like when you get there?
- What will be different than it is today when you get there? How will it be better than it is today?
- What have you done or accomplished to get there?
- How will you know if you are successful?
- How will people talk about this?
- What are potential barriers to that success? How can you overcome them?
- What types of things do you see need to be done to get there?
- What are possible first steps?

After we have formed a clearer vision, inviting "black hat" feedback—the questions that really challenge us on the details—helps us anticipate any potential organizational or even individual resistance we'll face once we start to move into action. Inviting this kind of thinking can help us reframe our ideas to be more successful by seeing potential blockers so that we can address them in order to stand a better chance of traction.

But don't give this privilege to just anyone.

The metaphor of birth is not one that all Catalysts can relate to, but when it comes to our idea-babies, it's too accurate to ignore. The process of bringing something new into the world is exciting, vulnerable, dangerous, and painful. Be kind to yourself. Giving someone free reign to critique—to tell you that your idea-baby is ugly—can sometimes be too much, too fast. You're presenting your new little baby idea that's wrapped up closely in your ego, in a completely vulnerable state.

Choose that person strategically and let them know they are in a position of honor: "We only chose three people to help us with this. We want you to be honest with us but maybe not brutally honest just yet because we literally just gave birth to this." If you've chosen well, those people will get it and will help you dig into the flaws without crushing your spirit. Other Catalysts are usually a safe bet for this, which is one reason why people enjoy our retreats and classes so much. It is a wonderful feeling to be able to show people your ideas when you are feeling vulnerable, then to be met with encouragement to make that vision bigger and better. No one shoots you down or says you're crazy.

When we are met with positivity, it boosts our confidence, while skepticism can kill our confidence.

In later chapters, we'll walk through the process of mapping your network to identify champions, safe challengers, translators, and supporters.

LEADING CHANGE: LISTENING TOURS

The first work that we do in vision is our own. Before the safe feedback, before the map, before drawing with our teams, we're synthesizing data and getting the dots connected on our own. But just because the connection happens in our head doesn't mean we vision in isolation. Active Listening was our first tool precisely because we can't create change alone. Depending on our context, a Listening Tour might be a starting point for all of the steps we just covered.

Leading change is all about creating buy-in with the people who will be affected by our implementing the vision. That's why we make it a point to not share too soon or too widely—you'll risk fueling your detractors or you'll scare away potential supporters. By sharing progressively, within concentric circles of safety, the vision continues expanding to more people the further refined it becomes, until eventually we're ready to show potential detractors. By that point, we've iterated on the vision so much that it's likely to be solid, and we're just getting that last level of fingerprints on it for the sake of buy-in. This is more or less the process of leading change that we'll step through in the next few chapters—Listening Tours first, then Co-creation Tours, and finally Feedback Tours.

The tools in each chapter facilitate improved leadership in each of these stages, but this tour in particular often comes at the very beginning of the process. Especially if you're in a new role or company, you might be connecting the dots, but the dots themselves don't really belong to you. Without direct feedback and active listening, you'll have no contextual awareness for the change itself.

One Catalyst described this process as *going on a Listening Tour*. She spent a few weeks in the new culture of the organization, from the ground level to the executive table, learning their language and hearing their concerns. Then she would draft a vision, beginning with direct impacts on the organization. This not only gave her data but also built a rapport with the people around her. People saw themselves and their objectives in the vision, which meant buy-in was there from the beginning.

The vision starts with you, but it's often the output of you going around to each person and team to listen deeply and assess the problems from their perspective.

Who you know matters, but even deeper than that, *who trusts you* matters. When you can listen deeply to someone about their concerns and opinions and world view, you build trust. And trust makes way for change in a way that no other strategy can.

Of course, the likelihood of being new in an organization is high for a Catalyst, and we don't always know who to go to at this stage. There are unspoken, intuitive pieces to the puzzle that you simply can't know without putting the time in. That's ok. You can still build partnerships with people who do have the network, or you can begin to create your own.[11]

Whether you have an existing network or are starting from scratch, a Listening Tour allows you to bring many perspectives in as the data that feeds the vision. We do not all see the world in the same way. To bring others into the world that we see as possible, we have to show it to them. If you've listened deeply to the concerns of people around you, then brought the right people on board at the right time, the vision will be a reflection of the group. When you move into action, it will be with their concerns and impact in mind.

That's why we pause to name and draft up a vision statement and Action Map. That's why we bring others on board. That's why we're gentle with ourselves and others along the way. Because the only way to usher the brilliant new thing into the world is together, with kindness. And clarity is kindness.

REJUVENATION PRACTICES TO FACILITATE VISION

Michael would tell you that he doesn't have strong rejuvenation practices, but his focus on purpose, meaning, and family is actually a powerful form of rejuvenation. Pausing to give himself time to come to a vision creates space for remarkable manifestation.

Rejuvenation practices are not about checking something off of your list but about sustaining your energy for the work ahead.

---

11 This article is incredibly helpful for a deeper analysis on this topic: Julie Battilana and Tiziana Casciaro, "The Network Secrets of Great Change Agents," *Harvard Business Review*, July–August 2013, https://hbr.org/2013/07/the-network-secrets-of-great-change-agents.

Michael's reminder to Catalysts? "You're here for a reason. You have a gift that someone else doesn't. Use it."

CREATE SPACIOUSNESS

So often, our society reduces the Catalyst's ability to vision to its consumable components. We find ourselves saying, "I need to sit down and build a deck," or "I've got to present this vision at a meeting at three," expecting to crank up our visioning on command. Just churn out something usable and move on to the next problem to solve.

But the heart of visioning is creativity. It's imagining and intuiting and building something new. When we try to compress the creative side of the process in order to force the production side of it—the strategy alone—we either dilute the ultimate vision or frustrate ourselves along the way. And yes, sometimes both.

If we don't know how to name what we need under ideal circumstances, we certainly don't know how to ask for it under pressure. Like our other strengths, we come to believe that a clear vision "just happens," and when it doesn't, we think we've lost our power. In reality, we've just compressed our process so much that there's no room for our brains to move like they need to.

Spaciousness is in short supply in our society, so we have to create it:

- *Get into nature.* Hold a meeting outside. Practice forest baths. Get your hands into garden dirt after work, or slip your shoes off to step into the grass on a lunch break.

- *Get back in your body.* Do yoga or meditations before meetings. Expand out of the default brain-only space into a deeper sense of mindfulness and awareness.
- *Shift your physical space.* Take walks with your team. Find non-traditional spaces like art galleries or vineyards to hold meetings. Use spaces where you can see nature.

Protect that spaciousness with your routines and your maps and your visions, and bring it into your organization in bold, powerful ways. Require it for vision work and model it in everyday work. Make space for your whole selves at the intersection of creativity and strategy, and you'll be surprised how much more good you'll be able to do in the world.

SEE YOURSELF IN YOUR VISION

Catalysts manifest. We bring things into existence. We have an insatiable hunger to make all parts of life better. But we don't have endless energy reserves to make that happen. We can map out the strongest visions and bring together the strongest supporters—*and*, if we don't pause now and then on the plateaus, we're not going to make it all the way up the mountain.

Where you spend your energy and the amount of energy you have available determines what you can amplify and create. It can't be said enough: put yourself on the Action Map, too. Use your natural skills and newly acquired tools to manifest the life that you want to lead—not just the external change you hope to create in the world. Whether you dream of a new city, deeper friendships, a romantic relationship, a shift in health, a more robust rejuvenation routine, be sure it ends up on your Action Map. When you know what rejuvenates you and helps to fill your energy tank, put it on your Action Map (and block it into your calendar). You have the power to manifest, so be sure to get crystal clear on all the things you want to manifest, especially for yourself.

Then, when you inevitably come short of the many goals, phantom goals, and big visions, give yourself some compassion. Give yourself permission to let things go. Give yourself permission to fail. The energy spent in guilt and shame will not make your vision any closer to reality. Let it go. Come back to your present reality and adapt. It's what you're great at. If we could give you one tool or gift to walk away with, it would be self-compassion. From there, everything else will flow.

WORK TOWARD FINANCIAL FREEDOM

Part of seeing yourself in the vision is seeing your future ability to pursue the new opportunities that might present themselves. Money is one of those taboo topics that people rarely want to talk about, alongside religion and politics, but we have seen and personally experienced how financial concerns can hold us back from chasing the Big Thing we *need* to create in the world. Just imagine what it would feel like if the money didn't matter!

Michael was far from the first or last Catalyst to see change enabled through financial freedom. We've seen younger Catalysts without a family and mortgage and responsibilities able to act more bravely than some of their Catalyst counterparts felt that they could, because the financial risk of losing that job wouldn't be as devastating. And we've seen more senior Catalysts, who have given themselves the gift of financial flexibility, able to chase their dreams more fully.

Listen, we're not financial experts (though there are some of those in the Catalyst community). But what we do know is that no matter where we are on our journey, it's worth taking some time to consider how your finances are going to super-charge you or hold you back.

If you're at an early stage in your career, think about financial planning now. It's never too early to start, and your future Catalyst self may send deep gratitude back to you for having set yourself up to chase your big dream.

If you're mid-career, maybe think about the steps you can take over the next year or two to both give yourself the cushion you would need to make a change, while leveraging your current role to get the skills, training, and experience you need to make the jump.

There's another taboo piece within the sticky topic of finances, which is about our sense of self-worth, our struggle to fully articulate our value, and the frequent disconnect between our drivers (making successful change) and the currency of most organizations. The correlation between high salaries and power in organizations isn't an accident. Money is how organizations communicate worth or value of work contributed. And we are hoping that as you start to stand in your power, rack up the wins, and learn how to communicate your value, you can help your manager and leaders see it, too. Being a Catalyst is *hard work*. And even if it doesn't feel like we have any other choice but to take that on, it doesn't mean we shouldn't be rewarded for the—sometimes personally crushing—work we do to lead an organization forward.

Take the time to articulate your wins and value. Get ready for your mid-year and end-of-year reviews in advance. Do the research. Find out what others around you in your company or across the industry are making. It can be hard for us to find perfect corollaries for the work we do, so get creative. Look for three other job titles that describe your role (or roles, more likely) and make the case for an equitable raise. The worst they can say is no, which also gives you some input on how the organization is valuing you.

And it's ok to do all of this while not knowing where you'll end up or how you might leverage the freedom you commit to giving your future self. Michael spent years building up his financial freedom, and now he's *building a frigging space station*.

Honestly, even the sky might not be your limit.

THE VISION TOOLBOX

☐ **Active listening.** Remember that this change is meant to create a better future, and the only way to know what that means is to listen to the people most affected by that future. Listen deeply and allow that feedback to shape your vision.

☐ **Say it out loud.** Pause to articulate the vision that becomes clear—draft it up as an early vision statement and say it out loud to someone you trust who won't be impacted by the vision.

☐ **Tap into creativity.** Spend time percolating and imagining iterations to the vision. Use your tactile, creative brain to look at the problem and vision in another way.

☐ **Create an Action Map.** Identify your starting and end points and key milestones along the way. You'll absolutely iterate on this later on, but it gives you clear steps to start with and helps you let go of phantom goals and tasks that won't serve the ultimate vision.

- ☐ **Make a Not Right Now list.** Allow all of your idea babies space to exist without turning them into phantom goals that will hold you back. You can come back to those later when you can give them more intention and focus.
- ☐ **Don't share too soon.** When you're ready to move into action, share a clear, visual representation of it to the people who need the information. Don't rush into sharing it before it's ready or to people who aren't ready for it, or you'll lose buy-in and fuel your detractors.
- ☐ **Open up to challenges.** Reach out to your trusted network to invite feedback and, sometimes, black hat questions.
- ☐ **Go on Listening Tours.** To help form your vision, go listen to stakeholders and understand their world view, challenges, and ideas.
- ☐ **Create spaciousness.** Create spaciousness for vision with open time, a refreshing or creative environment, and care for your whole self.
- ☐ **See yourself in the vision.** Don't forget to map your own spaciousness and creativity into your plans, and above all else, practice self-compassion.
- ☐ **Work toward financial freedom.** Money is the currency of value in organizations and the resource we need to create bigger change. It's never too early or too late to work toward the financial freedom that will enable bigger, bolder, catalytic visions.

CHAPTER 5

ACTION AND ORCHESTRATION

 After more than a decade in management and consulting, Shakeya was at burnout. It had taken a lot of travel, self-sacrifice, and advocating to exist in the role she was in, and the struggle had taken its toll. So when an opportunity to join an ethics and compliance department within an integrated health system became available, she was ready for the pivot. The excitement of something new, combined with the sense of purpose that came from an organization that wanted to make a difference for their patients and community, gave her the energy boost it seemed she needed.

The organization had an existing vision statement when she arrived and was accustomed to having their strategy plan articulated in a lengthy document. After a quick assessment, Shakeya identified several strategic activities that needed to change in order to activate the vision. And, in typical Catalyst fashion, she dove into them quickly. That's when the chatter started.

Shakeya recalls the shift from consultant to contributor as a difficult one: "When I was consulting, people selected me for a project because they knew I could come in quickly and transform their operations."

When she shifted to her new role, however, the average tenure was in the twenty- to twenty-five range and she lacked credibility. "The organization is relationship driven. Therefore, having me come in with limited relationships and limited trust it required me flex my typical approach to be effective in my role and drive lasting change."

There were external messages to battle. *She doesn't understand our organization. We're complicated. We don't move this fast. She needs to move this way, collaborate here, and follow that process.*

And there were internal gremlins, too. *What am I doing here, really? Can I actually be successful?*

Focusing on the wrong problems here could have quickly sent Shakeya back into burnout all over again.

Instead of trying to address the resistors individually, she went back to her advocate—the former client who brought her in and was now her boss—to find some balance within all of the noise. Her boss confirmed that she was in fact on the right track in spite of what peers, her team, and external stakeholders were saying, and that she was supported in whatever needed to happen. Not long after that, she connected with Catalyst Constellations and began to develop a strategy to achieve the vision in spite of her resistance.

The ultimate vision for the company had been right, and Shakeya's map to get there was spot on as well. What she really needed was to simplify it all into a unifying framework that fit within the larger vision of the company so that others could align to it.

Once she understood the company's strategy and identified their needs more thoroughly, she was able to turn the broader vision into a more specific ambition statement. It was that they would be enabled by technology, analytics, and reporting; supported by an ethical culture, not just a compliance culture; and attract and retain world-class talent. Then the department set the target date of 2020 to be recognized as one of the World's Most Ethical Companies™, because the achievement would be more tangible and celebratory than other measurements.

With the clearer path to accomplishing the vision, she shifted to an activation plan that could be easily followed. "I had to understand the strategy of the organization and where we fit into the bigger *why* of the organization, then isolate it to two or three things that everybody could mobilize around."

She created three pillars for each team to use as they worked toward the vision: people, systems, and affordability. What are we going to do to grow and develop our talent into world-class, energized contributors? How do we develop standards or centralized work for better efficiency? And how can we eliminate waste in the budget? This gave each team the freedom to develop their own plans around those pillars, so everyone could understand the role they play in the vision and adopt it. Together, they articulated their own visions and tracked progress toward them.

Shakeya could have gotten stuck where many of us do: we have a vision, but we start running toward it without fully articulating it so that people can follow. Instead, she simplified and articulated it in a way that built trust instead of eroding it. She came back to a place of clarity and empathy for the people on her team—as well as self-compassion as she found her way through—and that created spaciousness for out of the box thinking and a strategy that became clearer and clearer at each step.

Her boss affirmed her presence and vision, her true advocates and evangelists within the organization backed her up, and Catalyst Constellations supported her whole self along the way. And in 2019, her organization was named as one of the World's Most Ethical Companies™, a full year before their target date, without sacrificing anyone's well-being to do it.

SUPERPOWERS AND BLIND SPOTS

Catalysts are always *in* action, though we don't always *enact* the vision that we set out to realize. Action isn't just the steps toward solution, but toward refining the solution to the puzzle. We go on learning journeys, we research, we activate our community, we learn new problem-solving skills, we talk to customers...

These are all actions that can begin long before we have really started "creating" the solution. And once a vision is in place, the action only intensifies.

In the initial research to identify Catalysts, we found that for some, action was an unconscious step. Respondents said things like, "I see puzzle pieces coming together and am already solving it before others recognize there was even a puzzle in front of us" When we see what can be better, why *wouldn't* we move toward that future right away? To not press forward would be to deny the world of this thing that would make it better.

That shift into solutions is action, and it happens before we think twice. This is fearlessness and a superpower, worth giving yourself credit for—even if it feels natural.

Action can be difficult to bring to conscious competence. Sometimes, Catalysts lean into the label "ideas person" and leave more action-oriented words to others. Even as we drafted this chapter, we spun out around our definitions, because action can look different for each Catalyst.

Do small movements still count as action?

Are the things we do to gain feedback action, too?

Is it action if the results are intangible?

The answer we came to is *yes*—to both. Action is about forward movement, regardless of the intended outcome.

Presenting the idea for feedback is action. Workshopping is action. Pulling a team together to orchestrate, testing hypotheses, and prototyping are all forms of action.

When we look at it that way, it's easier to see how much action we're taking in any given moment. The same fearlessness that gives us power turns into a lack of prioritization and focus when we don't rein it in. Where someone else might struggle to identify something worth pursuing, we start moving without realizing it's happened.

In the last chapter, we talked about how easy it is for all of our ideas to turn into phantom goals that we hold ourselves to. Those same goals can take up energy if we're not careful to prioritize them.

Even worse, our speed and tenacity can seriously hamper our ability to orchestrate. Few Catalysts consider orchestration a superpower at all—many of us struggle once it's time to get everyone on board and moving in the same direction. If we had a literal orchestra to lead, it might look like sketching out half of a composition with shorthand and personal notes for the music in our head, then expecting the band to play along.

Fortunately, the emotional intelligence and empathy that allows us to read a room and pick up on subconscious data cues serve as a superpower to counter what we struggle with here. That pause and intentionality is substantially more effective than when we assume someone already saw what we saw or assume that they're going to follow us.

Plans, priorities, and good orchestration facilitate and sustain action. The tools included here will help make those steps easier—on both yourself and your team.

PAUSE WITH SHANNON

I was much more aware of my hyper-catalytic qualities when I started my new role at Ericsson. I very consciously leveraged tools to support my ability to bring my team along.

My first big action was co-creating the vision with the entire team within the first thirty days (in a beautiful location, with a relaxed dinner both nights, a graphic recorder to support our work). There was so much wisdom on the team, over two hundred years of company experience, from different aspects of the business. We identified both a high-level vision for the team as well as a number of specific solutions we would end up pursuing.

From that initial workshop, I created a priority list for myself (and thus the team), which stayed on the whiteboard next to my desk in the open workspace. I move fast. I can pivot without intention or communication if I'm not mindful. My priority list (including one item dedicated to personal rejuvenation) was always available as a reminder to myself as I came into the office every day but also for my team. A personal and team accountability tool—if someone came to me with a project for consideration, we could have a discussion about where it fit in the priorities and if something needed to shift.

As we continually updated and refined the vision, I made sure my leadership team had regular offsites where we could create the space and time to bring in deeper thinking and the spaciousness needed to both iterate on our vision and have the difficult conversations needed when you're creating change.

Finding locations where we could be more inspired and creative—whether it was our startup space in the city or a hotel near the ocean—was important. Equally important was creating spaciousness and downtime in the agenda—not easy for a highly catalytic leader. But that open time combined with an inspired location allowed us to get away from the tyranny of the urgency experienced in the office. We could be more reflective and thoughtful. We constantly revisited and refined the vision, examined the new information we had learned from the actions we had taken since our last offsite, and explored what we needed to iterate in the next quarter.

Recognizing that change is hard, I focused on what I consider key skills for a Catalyst team, starting with self-awareness. (Sound familiar?)

We started by looking at each individual's personal drivers. Having them imagine back into their family history to understand where and how they may have inherited their personal values, beliefs, and sense of purpose. The team then compared their own values with those reported by the team about the team. We identified the gaps and co-created the values we wanted to collectively embody.

We introduced how the brain works in connection with other people and emotions (mirroring neurons, the brain under stress, etc.). Using mindfulness and presencing exercises, we had the team explore the different ways of listening (brain, heart, will—all tied to *Theory U*). We developed active listening skills combined with empathy so that the team could learn how to work at peak performance together as well as across the organization.

I had the team do energy audits to track at each offsite where they were charged and where they were losing energy across four areas (body, emotions, mind, and spirit).

All in an effort to continually develop self-awareness and empathy to help us navigate being a highly catalytic team.

While I tried to support my hyper-catalytic nature, there were places where I struggled. I was exhausted from talking about the strategy. I was frustrated. I was chomping at the bit to get on to more execution and speed up the projects that were in flight. I definitely *believed* I was over-communicating to ensure that the entire team was bought in on the vision that I saw so clearly. But clearly there was a disconnect.

During one team meeting, where I was sharing the final "official" strategy we were pursuing, I opened it up for Q&A after the presentation. *Silence.* I decided to keep explaining more details for twenty minutes—keeping the meeting open so people had time to process and ask questions. *Silence.* I left assuming everyone understood. Only later did I find out that while people broadly understood the vision, they were still unclear on how to operationalize the strategy. In hindsight, I should have spent more time one-on-one with my direct reports ensuring they were clear on the details of their team's next steps towards realizing the vision.

Throughout my career, I have been fortunate to have team members who were both catalytic and able to support my weaker areas. I truly believe that a team diverse in skill sets, approaches, and experiences makes the whole team stronger. I had intentionally hired for diversity in many different traits: gender, race, industry experience and tenure, analytic/strategic capabilities vs. designing and making. I even created an excel spreadsheet tracking all the various attributes to ensure my natural affinities didn't influence my hiring in one direction! But on one team offsite, we had my direct reports use the Belbin Team Roles evaluation, and we realized we had no "Completer Finishers" on the test. That's not good at all for a highly catalytic team.

I hired an amazing group of leaders with whom I had high trust and could easily delegate. I knew that they would both execute and ask questions or push back when they disagreed. This becomes even more import-ant as we tackle the hard task of driving change into an organization.

Whether it's leveraging someone's Salesforce skills to track the team's impact to the bottom line of all our efforts or another's great operational skills to map out all the processes and stakeholder maps, being able to get a clear view of the system and the resistance helps me and the team go back to the Vision, Action, Iteration plan with intentionality and data.

There are different ways Catalysts can delegate to gain support and a more mindful approach. Working with a personal or team coach is also a great way to delegate some of the energetic and strategy work. Over the years, I've had the great opportunity to work with people like Tracey and my team coach, Ashley Munday. Finding people who can provide a safe place for me and my team to process, troubleshoot, work around some of my own catalytic blind spots, and reconnect with my own and my team's areas of strength always helps.

In my current role, I feel very fortunate to have such a fantastic Co-Founder and Co-CEO. Tracey and I complement each other's strengths so well. And where there are areas that neither of us shine, we have enough wisdom now to hire badass people to support us.

ACTION TOOLS

We (and our bosses) sell ourselves short if we think implementation is all that matters. If we freeze frame a Catalyst to look for action points, we'll find them in the mania of data-gathering almost constantly. It happens when perfecting the vision, when bringing others together to realize the vision, across every stage of iteration, and all the way up until the final project is manifested or handed off for someone else to implement. Your role as Catalyst won't necessarily include those final steps at all. Instead, it's often synthesizing data, turning it into a mapped vision, and getting enough people on board to make it reality—while you move on to the next challenge and leave behind an organization who sees and appreciates your value.

If we continue to stretch the mental muscles required to pause, then we can create space to see action points, facilitate them, and make them visible for stakeholders as well. It significantly helps us define and articulate our value.

CREATE PRIORITIZATION LISTS

When we spotted action in the tools for the last chapter, it was in the Action Map and Not Right Now List, which is a kind of prioritization list that keeps us moving toward the bigger vision. Making everyday lists outside of the Action Map is another way to stop phantom goals and iteration spirals in their tracks.

Lists help us think about what we're doing instead of just barreling into motion. They give extra idea babies a place to live outside of our heads without feeling obligated to pursue them. They keep us from forgetting what's truly important (or could be important later). They help us cross the Ts and dot the Is that we might not otherwise see when we jump straight into action, and they help us get realistic about our time.

When we intentionally prioritize our actions, it allows us the fluidity we love without unintentionally spinning out into left field. And lists are the best way to fiercely prioritize our ideas and actions. They make us hyper-focused on what we should do (making us more successful) and clearer on what we should say no to (helping to keep us from burning out).

Hang onto your Action Map list and reference it often. Make priority lists for each step on that map. Make a list in the morning for everything you'd like to do, then evaluate that list in the evening to capture what actually got done.

If you're able to set aside a Not Right Now list, the next step is to *actually* stop yourself from doing those things right now. Shakeya is brilliant at prioritization and reminds her Catalyst cohorts that, "'No' is a complete sentence." When two things are important to drive toward and seven things would be nice, don't fall into the trap of guilt, shame, or frustration that the seven aren't happening yet. That doesn't mean our goals have to be rigid.

The obvious concern here is that stopping to work on lists and checking in so frequently with ourselves will keep us from the work that makes change happen—and a change not realized can be painful for Catalysts.

In fact, we sometimes turn that Not Right Now list into a Why Haven't I Yet? list. The phantom goals feel so real that we experience shame for not pursuing them.

How tightly have you held onto your mental list of every vision that became clear, every solution that needs to be implemented, and every change that hasn't been made? How many times have you berated yourself for coming up short?

That's not the kind of list we're advocating for here. We're not asking you to bring pauses, rejuvenation, and clarity into your process just so that you have another thing to hang onto or to turn into judgment and shame.

In an article about clarity, Deepak Chopra frames prioritization as a matter of mindfulness: "The settled mind, in fact, is the most capable of meeting the day's demands because it is guided from within...The biggest question you can ask yourself comes down to a very simple one: What shall I do today? Why am I here now in this moment?"

Magical thinking lies to us about what we should be able to do until we lose ourselves trying. Acknowledge to yourself now that you literally cannot do everything that you envision as possible, especially not all at once. Prioritize what needs to happen right now and set the rest aside. Give yourself permission to relinquish some of those amazing ideas, with intention and purpose, until you have space to pick up some of them again, one at a time.

Prioritization lists will not be effective if they are about obligation or guilt. Think of them as a way to externalize all of the things bouncing around in your head, to then hold up against reality. That framing turns lists into incredibly effective data points that help us prioritize and streamline our action more effectively.

REGULAR REFLECTION

As we'll see in the next chapter, iteration happens almost simultaneously with action. In most cases, we jump into action precisely because we need more data to help us iterate toward a clearer objective. Rather than jumping reactively into that new action as soon as that feedback comes in, a constant practice of prioritization helps us take each action with intention. Does the data show me that this idea is still worth pursuing? Is it an idea that I should come back to in six months, given what the data is telling me?

Prioritization skills necessarily include zooming out now and then to acknowledge what you've actually done and to pivot toward where your focus would be better served. We do this not only to stay on track with what we're manifesting but to give ourselves credit for actions that we might otherwise leave unnoticed.

For the Catalyst who is prone to swim outside of their lane without support structures to allow it, we might also need to reflect on where we're stepping into action and whether it's an effective use of our time, energy, and influence. In *The Seven Habits of Highly Effective People*, Stephen Covey encourages us to focus proactively only on what we can control. While it might be concerning to see that the CEO doesn't have a strong vision, that's outside of an individual contributor's sphere of control. Stepping outside of that sphere, especially if you do so frequently, will strip the influence you have within that sphere. Similarly, staying within it and creating wins with the people and processes that you can directly affect will build the trust you need to expand your influence and control over time.

Daily reflection on what you did from moment to moment creates a literal freeze frame on that super-speed superhero state that we tend to fall into. Sure, it felt like a whirlwind, but what happened in the midst of it? Did you feel like nothing got done because you truly dropped the ball, or did you drop one ball because you successfully juggled seventeen more?

We also need to look up now and then to check in with the original vision—have I shifted back into old habits I was trying to avoid, do I still want to pursue this objective, am I spending my time as efficiently as I could be to make that thing happen? Am I getting distracted with things that are outside of my influence that I actually cannot control?

Reflection is the bridge between action and iteration that can keep us tied to the original vision, while keeping us in line with our priorities and realistic about our time and abilities. Taking time to reflect on the impacts of Action makes Iteration more successful and helps bring others along more effectively.

GET IT IN YOUR CALENDAR

Unless you're in billable-hours land, it's easy for the Catalyst to make "priorities" and never realize just how unrealistic they are. We could block out our time, ruminate on tasks, force ourselves to focus, get rigid about time, push those two actions to that one Friday even though we're also going to be at Disneyland that day...

Or, more practically, we can just get strategic about when we make the lists themselves.

Start with your list of to-dos in the morning, being intentional about what goals you're working toward and listing out the great things you're choosing to set aside for another time. Then at the end of the day, go back to that same list. What did you actually get done? What took up the bulk of the day when you thought it would take less? What do you need to write in as extraneous things you tackled, and do those things clue you in on what should be prioritized tomorrow?

While you're tracking, pay attention to which activities are giving you energy versus those that you find depleting. You may be able to delegate some of these things you dislike—in fact, you may need to. Let's be honest, it takes us more time to do the things we dread. But someone else may actually love the very things we hate. By tracking the energy tied to our activities and delegating those that will probably take longer (if they ever get completed at all), we can help manage not just our time, but our energy.

If we get realistic about what we actually have time to accomplish, the less likely our magical thinking will take hold in the future. Build the habit of writing down your priorities aligned to your vision and Action Map, then ensure there is time dedicated in your calendar to work toward those things. As you reflect on what's listed compared with what's actually happening, you can begin to combat magical thinking and reduce burnout.

We can't pour from an empty vessel. We know this, but none of it matters to us as long as we feel like we're making progress towards our vision. We're *really* good at this part—the "trying to cram all of our big ideas into unrealistic space and time" part. But having a better handle on time helps us prioritize the rejuvenation that makes our work possible—the more hours we work, the higher our likelihood of diminishing returns.[12]

The antidote is to become more mindful about that progress and the time that it takes. By getting proactive in prioritization—and holding rejuvenation practices in high regard on the calendar as well—that inevitable moment of burnout doesn't have to come as soon, as frequently, or as hard. We think better, work better, lead better, and make change better when we create spaciousness for our whole selves to thrive.

---

12   Researcher John Pencavel from Stanford University found that fifty hours is our optimal max work week. Anything more and we hit diminishing marginal returns. Research here: John Pencavel, "The Productivity of Working Hours," (discussion paper, Stanford University and IZA, April 2014), http://ftp. iza.org/dp8129.pdf.

ORCHESTRATION TOOLS

Catalysts are magical in their own way, but when we start to drift into magical thinking and time-bending antics, it becomes a problem for the people around us. There's something transcendent that happens when we see the vision for the future. We see it so clearly that it feels like we're there already. It's just an arm's length away. The jolt back to reality, when we have to orchestrate other people to get there, is disorienting.

When we move too quickly into action or through cycles of iteration, we can create a sense of quicksand for the people around us. We don't intentionally miss orchestration—we forget it, because we assume that everyone else can see the potential future state as clearly as we can. It comes to us so palpably that there's no way, in our minds, that anyone could have missed it.

The tools we've already covered can help us avoid the biggest pitfalls of orchestration. When we pause long enough to paint a picture of the vision to the right people at the right time, there are fewer surprises. Action Maps help us lay a bridge between where we are and where we're going, and it's easier for people to follow us when the path is clear. When we're clear on our priorities and realistic about time, we ask less of our people. We create less quicksand.

To be fair to ourselves, sometimes orchestration is difficult because we're taking actions that have literally not been taken before. We're trailblazers who are going where few to none have gone before. In that context, what feels like little tweaks to us might take a year to come to fruition. Be kind to yourself as you catalyze through uncharted waters—and use these tools and practices to be kind to the people around you as well.

NETWORK MAP

Network maps help us identify the context we're playing in. If an Action Map shows us the steps we think we need to take to get to the ultimate change, Network Maps help us better understand the system and actors that will help us make that change happen. Who will be on your side as an endorser? Who has the power to make decisions? Are there active resistors to be aware of, who you'll need to be more careful with? Where are there general influencers to create positive flow with?

It's worth noting here that we're often in contexts where we have no idea what the network is like. In a powerful HBR piece titled "Exerting Influence without Authority," Professor Jay A. Conger is quoted as saying this about building a network: "Certain people are portals to other people—they can connect you to more and bigger networks...build relationships with these individuals in particular."[13] We don't have to have the full network in place already—we just have to find the people who do.

A more difficult challenge is presented when we realize that we've damaged our influence in our eagerness to make change. What we see as connections and systems change, others see us as swimming outside of our lane. We threaten people who are invested in the status quo and exhaust others who only experience us as sources of criticism.

A Network Map can point to connections where we have influence, need to build influence with someone we're not already in relationship with, or where we need to repair

---

13   Lauren Keller Johnson, "Exerting Influence Without Authority," *Harvard Business Review*, February 28, 2008, https://hbr.org/2008/02/exerting-influence-without-aut.

damage done to restore influence. Knowing who those people are and what they're connected to helps us know where to turn when the change requires it.

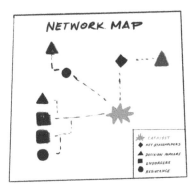

The Catalyst model of influence is adapted from the work of professors Allan R. Cohen and David L. Bradford in their book *Influence Without Authority*. The six-step influence model that they've created walks an individual through the process of establishing influence with someone based on the law of reciprocity—the belief that all of the positive and negative things we do for (or to) others will be paid back over time. This frame helps us remember that at the simplest levels, we're exchanging value. This is absolutely our experience and what we see playing out for Catalysts. The longer we're in one organizational context, the more we deliver on what we say we're going to do, the more influence and positive relationships we have. On the other hand, the more critical we are without orchestration toward the transformation, the less people trust us and want to hear from us.

We have developed a similar influence model aligned with the blind spots that trip us up in orchestration:

- Align your clarified vision with your goals for that person. What do you hope to get out of that interaction? Without being clear on your goals with that person and with the change you're trying to create, there's nothing to influence or orchestrate.
- Consider your current relationship with that person, especially if it's contentious. Understand the level of empathy, self-compassion, and resilience needed to work toward influence in that context.
- Assume ally-ship, best intentions, and a shared goal of coming to a great outcome. This step can be hard, especially if you have had previous conflict. Catalysts need to bring consciousness to our desired future state *and* a realistic view of the present before stepping into an attempted influence relationship with them.
- Diagnose their worldview and currencies. At work, what does their boss care about, what does their part of the organization reward? Personally, what are they energized by, and what motivates and rewards them? Do they want notoriety or anonymity? These are all factors that can help you create wins and avoid significant losses for them.
- Consider their relationship to the change you're making. Remember that it's difficult for people to adapt to any change, much less to the scale that we're often advocating. How might this change benefit them? Or possibly harm them in some way? Be especially aware of something that might threaten their role or eliminate part of their work.
- Build influence through give and take. With full clarity on not only your vision but how this person is both affected by and can affect the process of shaping and implementing the vision, you can begin to create influence with that person.

We've all been shut down before, and we'll probably get shut down again. But if we come into the conversation with defensiveness, there's no way we're going to build influence. Trust the vision, and work to turn that trust into a bridge between you.

If you feel resistance rising, shift your goal from convincing to curiosity. Why are they resisting? Is there something you don't see? What are their goals? How do you help them win, too?

Finally, remember this is an iterative process. We are *building* influence, and it can take time. Eventually, when you understand who that person is and what matters to them, it will inform how you talk with them about the vision. It will inform how you extend the invitation to them, and it will shape their support of you and overall influence within the organization.

And remember you won't win everyone over! So bring awareness (versus problem solving skills) to what is actually unfolding and possible with each stakeholder.

OVERCOMMUNICATION

When you first bring an idea forward to someone, there's a process they have to go through before they can accept it. The Transtheoretical Model of Change (TTM) breaks this down for us, showing that we move through three steps before action even starts (Prochaska & DiClemente). They are pre-contemplation, contemplation, preparation, *then* action, typically correlated with the respective responses *no, maybe, what's the plan*, and finally, *let's go*.

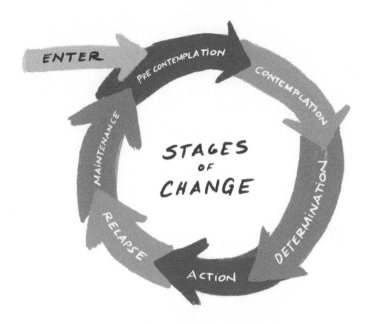

When we considered the necessity of empathy in chapter 2, these levels of internal processing layered almost directly onto cycles of grief. Resistance isn't just a refusal of the idea or the Catalyst but a way to self-protect against loss. Over-communicating at every step of the way gives people the opportunity to have their own experience, settle in, and hope-fully shift to the next stage.

From a Catalyst's perspective, we often experience people around us moving through the stages of change mapped out in the TTM like this: First, we share an idea, but no one seems to notice. Then eventually the idea becomes familiar to them, but they don't like it. They get annoyed that we're pushing them into discomfort. Eventually, they see value and wish the company had resources to pull it off, and somewhere down the line it's accepted, prioritized, and implemented as though it was always going to happen.

Catalysts move through those phases of change quickly, even though we're often experiencing the same mental shifts. Having empathy for that slower version of the process, and demonstrating that empathy by listening and bringing people along, becomes an early entry point to that pre-contemplation stage. It introduces the potential idea that maybe, possibly your idea might not be so bad. Overcommunicating your idea isn't pedantic—it's a necessary step to help others follow you across the bridge to that envisioned future as their relationship to your vision shifts each time they hear it again.

BREADCRUMBING

When an image or clip goes viral, the original context is often lost to the rest of the world. All we know is the cute face or funny phrasing, with no idea of where it actually began or who the person in that image actually is.

Viral might seem like a strong word for where your vision can go, but the principle remains. When that idea takes off and is ultimately implemented, it's often without the original context. You and your team won't necessarily be connected to it anymore.

When we ask Catalysts to breadcrumb, we're thinking of the story of Hansel and Gretel and how they leave breadcrumbs behind them to create a trail they could follow home. Not only do we want to leave a trail for other people to follow toward us into action, but we'd also like them to track the change back to us once the vision is "home." This isn't so we can get credit or accolades but to proactively keep a record of what we've done so that we can better articulate our value.

What we do looks like magic, but as we're increasingly seeing, it only takes a quick pause to see that's not true. There's a lot of behind-the-scenes work that goes into the changes we're able to bring into the world, and we need to bring them to consciousness first for ourselves, then for our organizations. Because we tend to be future and externally focused, it is not intuitive (or energy giving) to look behind us. We struggle here for similar reasons that we struggle to celebrate—we don't hate celebrating, but we also don't think about doing it.

Breadcrumbing gives us an answer when we inevitably get that question, "Can you help us track your impact?"

It is a muscle we need to build, less out of ego and desire for credit, and more to be understood for the value we bring to the organization and how it unfolds over time. It helps make that action that can feel invisible more visible.

While useful and necessary, breadcrumbing asks us to document that work when we'd rather leave it up to shorthand or unconscious competence, neither of which the organization will understand, recognize, or value. It's like being asked to show your long form work on the math problem you just solved in your head; the teacher needs to understand the rigor behind the work, to demonstrate that you didn't just "magic" the answer.

This can be painful for Catalysts. Who wants to document all the work we did? That's slow and boring and we want to poke our eyes out. But building this muscle actually makes our visions more *believable*. It feels odd when someone says with surprise, "Oh, you spoke with forty customers before you connected those dots with the industry research?" You may have spoken with forty customers, because you *always* speak with customers—who doesn't? But you're a Catalyst, and some of your steps aren't obvious or commonplace to other stakeholders. Articulating things that didn't feel like "action" not only give you credibility, but they tie a direct link to the fact that the idea originated with you.

Recognition and ego will be different drivers for different Catalysts. But for most, documenting the work so that we can claim credit feels uncomfortable. We mostly don't do this change thing for the recognition. We do it because it feels like it *has* to be done. All we care about is that the change is manifested in the world, whether or not we stick around to see it completed. Yet it's precisely because we largely don't stay until the work crosses the finish line that we need to breadcrumb.

Breadcrumbing can feel disingenuous when you're tying the ultimate win back to yourself when you kicked it off—it can feel like trying to claim credit for all those you galvanized to help get it done. Acknowledge and remember that new solution wouldn't exist without you. And, as we're seeing, it's hard work successfully getting everyone to the point where they were onboard and driving it to completion. You did that work, and the recognition you get, while maybe not something you covet, gives you the permission, the trust in your abilities, and thus the support you'll need when you go on to tackle the next even bigger challenge. So don't do it for you...do it for all the future change you want to create in the world.

When we use the tools that build out vision and action with more intention, breadcrumbing starts at the very beginning. The trail of mindful communication, clear representations of the vision, documentation of our actions, and the engaged network support we've earned will lead directly from the incredible change we manifest and the incredible catalytic mind that spawned it. It helps organizations see you and your process, with the clarity that you're coming to in the Catalyst Formula. And the best part? It creates more buy-in along the way.

LEADING CHANGE: CO-CREATION TOURS

Listening Tours help us get the lay of the land in the first thirty to sixty days, to identify the win for everyone before you form your initial vision. Co-Creation Tours actively involve people in refining that vision and building the path to implementation. It's a generative process, where we set out a general pathway, then bring key doers together with all of their collective wisdom to shape that pathway toward the bigger, better future together.

Like Listening Tours, this isn't a linear process that places this step after the other tools have been implemented. To be successful, you will have already done a Listening Tour that shaped a vision that appears to be a win for everyone. Your safe inner circle of Catalysts will have helped you hone it, and it will have enough legs to stand against resistors—without being so rigid that it can't change. The intent of this tour is to test out those legs and make sure that the wins are real.

Co-creation Tours are an opportunity to have a broader group of stakeholders contribute to the vision, as well as have them begin to take ownership to make that vision real. As we saw with Shannon, after just thirty days of a Listening Tour, she was able to bring her entire team into a co-creation session where the collective wisdom of over two hundred years of company and industry experience crafted a vision and Action Map to achieve that vision together.

But a Co-Creation Tour doesn't mean necessarily just one meeting. To increase the buy-in across the organization, you can host multiple Co-Creation sessions. Bring in the Operations leaders, the legal team, HR, salespeople, and customers. The scope of your vision will dictate who you need to include, but the more that people get to either insert their wisdom or their wins, the more robust the vision will be, and the most supporters you'll have along the journey.

Listening to all these multiple viewpoints doesn't mean you have to dilute your initial vision—it should actually help you shape the vision into something more tangible and real. Listen for the big wins that your co-creators need, while identifying supporters and possible resistors during your sessions. And as Catalysts, one of our superpowers is our ability to connect the dots and synthesize the wins in a meaningful way for the organization. The Co-Creation Tour puts those powers on full display. After all, if we're not there to do the most good, then we probably won't be successful and aren't focused on the right things.

Once you've included your stakeholders in the co-creation process, a great way to know if they're following you is to ask them to come back to you with *their* implementation plan. What are they going to do differently starting tomorrow, now that they understand the vision? This includes any updated goals or metrics. This gets you multiple data points—the metrics they're following, their connection with your vision, and actual input that could make the vision better.

When people get to participate in the co-creation process, it makes them feel like their voice is being heard.

They begin to see themselves in the vision, before we start to ask them for action. Prioritization and orchestration tools are going to pivot them toward implementation, and it's vital to know that they have buy-in or are at least wrestling with buy-in before we ask them to act.

Design thinking tools and any existing organizational tools for change can become helpful at this stage. You're often working with decades of collective experience, and it's beneficial for everyone to draw on those perspectives to shape a stronger vision.

Recently, after a group class on orchestration, one Catalyst spoke up about the speed of action and iteration, and how she was prone to "check the box" once a meeting had occurred. She reached out, had the conversation, and could move on. But the Co-Creation Tours that we do when leading change aren't about checking the box to unlock the next steps. The difference between that experience compared with the experience of actively listening to people, co-creating with them, and valuing their feedback, is palpable. She shared that pausing to be present in that interaction, and to check on whether that person really understood and was ready to be brought along, helped her avoid the glassy eyes and empty nod. It pivoted her toward true co-creation.

REJUVENATION WITHIN ACTION AND ORCHESTRATION

A key part of Shakeya's process was establishing trust with the people she worked with, since she was new on the scene, both in the industry and that organization, with big ideas for change. But even when the early chatter had tipped toward resistance, she made sure the vision was clear enough that anyone could follow it into implementation, and she created big wins as a result.

Shakeya made a concerted effort to be empathetic and understanding while leading the organization through serious change. She acknowledged the level of work on everyone's plate on a day to day basis and kept visioning work applicable and easy to digest. She created ten-minute vignettes around the components of the vision, such as a video of her boss explaining what trust means. She used those brief interludes to connect teams to the larger work at hand.

She also made a point to acknowledge failure as a natural process of action and iteration. In doing so, she discovered a narrative around perfection that needed to be broken: when she started acknowledging her failures, her team was almost happy about it.

For all of our iterative resilience, Catalysts can be incredibly hard on ourselves. Others perceiving joy in our failure, or learning that someone had been unintentionally hurt or left behind is painful, especially when we deeply believe that vision is intended for a higher good. Criticism of our ideas feels like criticism of ourselves, and it can echo the harsh criticism that we often internalize on a daily basis.

When resistance chatter turned to self-judgment, criticism, and shame in her own mind, it took more than just influence models and tactical tools to get Shakeya through this orchestration. Rejuvenation practices and regular, intentional pauses kept her going.

She started gardening, taking more time to listen to jazz, and connected with her favorite people. She started to get clear on what she was saying *yes* to, then began to say *no* to other things so she had time to build clarity and resilience.

With some distance, it became clear that it wasn't her *failure* that they were relieved to see but her *humanity*. They had shaped a story around how unbreakable she was because they didn't know how much she beat herself up on the inside.

Once she and her boss started talking about places where they missed the mark or failed, it gave them permission to embrace failure as well. Hand in hand with failure, they could also celebrate success. "At one event, we had people dress up in black tie attire—it was like the Oscars. Our internal audit team secured the award results in a briefcase. We had presenters read the award details and announce the winners. After the formal event, we had an after party. It was a sense of overwhelming success."

When she brought her failures into the light, it accomplished multiple things. It gave individuals permission to own their own missteps. It built trust in leadership. And it also quieted stories about perfection that both Shakeya and the team had been telling themselves. She didn't take this step lightly, either. In fact, she made an agreement with herself within her process and made sure to leave a clause for self- compassion:

> If I violate this agreement, I will be kind to myself. I will not invoke judgment or shame, because I understand that every second I'm given in this life is an opportunity to start over in my pursuit.

"We get beaten up so much from others," she reminds us. "Let's not beat ourselves up, too."

This level of self-compassion is what Shakeya needed to return from burnout, even more than the exciting new vision. She now articulates her rejuvenation practice as **The Joy Equation: Clarity + Purpose x Tribe = Joy**. Without intending to, Shakeya has her new passion, bringing this message to people: that connecting to your purpose and to people in all areas of life creates joy. When she gets up in front of an audience to talk about The Joy Equation, she both embodies the joy she's advocating for while bringing people to tears, because they finally remember to find their joy. She is *that* clear on the transformational potential of The Joy Equation.[14]

"You need clarity, which means you need to have stillness. You need to welcome peace and silence. Whether you want joy or not, you need space to get clear about what's happening. Take

---

14   Shakeya McDow, "The Joy Equation," https://catalystconstellations.com/insights/the-joy-equation.

a beat, or you'll fall into those cyclical habits again. Once you get clear, all of the other stuff will line up."

DEMONSTRATE EMPATHY (YES, AGAIN AND AGAIN)

Ignoring the impact of change on the people around us will stall action, every time. Underlying nearly every tool is a layer of empathy that makes it work. Network maps are useful for strategy, but empathy allows us to build influence. Action Maps give us a path, but empathy helps us share them safely.

Empathy rests on our ability to both deeply, actively listen and on our own self-awareness, which allows us to be fully present for others. When we spend a few mindful moments contemplating the reality of the situation (not just how we want to perceive it) and how it might be impacting others, we can develop a deep sense of empathy.

Don't just ask what they think about the plan. Ask them how you can support them and their team. Ask how you might unintentionally get in their way. Find out how you can best work together and what you can do to make their world better.

The trust that you build through empathy becomes the trust that they'll have as they leap off the cliff toward your proposed change.

We recently hosted Charlene Li, author of five books, including the *New York Times* bestseller, *Open Leadership*, as a speaker within a Catalyst Constellations event. She reminded us that we don't have to tell anyone we're problem-solvers—simply ask them what their biggest challenges are and then tell them you can solve them.

Our chances of successfully manifesting change that impacts a group of people skyrockets when we're able to interlace that change with empathy in this way. If someone feels like you're empathetic to them and sees it in the way you listen to them and take their feedback to heart, odds are, they're going to work with you.

Empathy shifts the balance away from defensiveness, pushiness, and moving quickly on the vision in our own heads. It allows us to listen deeply and work thoughtfully with the people around us to create mutual wins.

Knowing your people, utilizing your network, and moving people through a change process requires a deep working knowledge of both your people and yourself. It requires a fair amount of self-awareness to know just how much ambiguity and change you and others around you can take. The people who start off as your biggest supporters might distance themselves the more uncomfortable it gets, and those who might have been detractors can surprise you. There are significant emotional shifts that happen along the path to change, and that can come with shifts in acceptance and support as well. While you might have a beautifully mapped network on the outset, or for a different set of changes, give your people some of their own spaciousness to adapt to what you're asking of them.

DELEGATE TO SUPPORT YOUR STRENGTHS

Catalysts maintain energy for action well when we partner with people who enjoy tackling the work that drains us. The closer we get toward implementation, the less interest most of us have in seeing it through. It can consume energy without ever giving anything back, and that can feel impossible to overcome.

There are absolutely detail-oriented Catalysts in the world, so this might not necessarily translate one-to-one. However, we all have tasks that make us feel alive and tasks that spin us right down into that pit of burnout.

If you're in a position to hire someone—from a new employee to a contracted virtual assistant to an agency—or to partner up with a peer, do it. Remembering Shannon's cautionary tale about her team full of Catalysts without any "Completer Finishers," we all have a role to play in the execution of a big change. Seek out teams with a diverse range of skills that will support your strengths as a Catalyst while you support their efforts toward change. You don't have to have an existing team to make that network come together, either.

If this feels frustratingly slow and inefficient, we understand. It's hard to acknowledge that we need other people when we're sure we can do it faster or better alone. Even if you feel like you can handle everything on your plate right now, consider the bus theory: If you were to be hit by a bus tomorrow, would you want progress to stop?

If you're dedicated to making positive change in the world, you *have* to bring other people along with you. Yes, we can wrestle through some things on our own. Even our biggest actions are sometimes completed faster when we do them on our own. But just because we *can* doesn't mean we *should*. If you are losing energy to tasks that someone else can do, you aren't serving the bigger purpose, and it won't be sustainable. Let it go.

PAUSE AND RE-GROUND WITH THE FORMULA

Slowing down can be uncomfortable for the Catalyst. Stopping to bring others on board, to create spaciousness, to finally give ourselves a break for once—that can feel almost painful. We want to keep moving. For each of us, that discomfort around slowing or stopping can stem from a number of different causes: fear, worry, past trauma, or even excitement and anxiousness to see the vision realized. We have an insatiable hunger to make change, met by an increasing concern that people aren't getting it and we might not see it realized. That's not a great place for an action-oriented person to be.

In our world, when action means results and results mean worth and the Catalyst entangles all of that with personal value—what happens when you can't make the result come to life? Or, even more frustratingly: what if you don't even *want* to be the person to see it through to realization?

Our go-get-it culture teaches us to tie our personal worth to what we are able to *accomplish*, especially on behalf of others. Today, that looks like the work that we do and the money we're paid for it. It's the deliverables—the vision in hand, the enacted plans, the measurable outcomes—not the input. So as Catalysts, we often minimize our "dot-connecting," intangible action, and underlying skills as magic because we don't know how else to quantify it within that system.

Ground yourself to the vision, become mindful about how you step into action and bring others along, iterate with purpose, and hold space for it all with rejuvenation. This formula serves your team just as much as it serves you. The more efficiently you work in the action and orchestration phase, the more likely you'll see the vision realized. Understanding the magic in your hands helps you realize it's not just magic after all.

Before you spin out into indefinite iteration cycles, understand that you won't be able to pull rabbits out of this hat forever. Your mind and body have a limit. Give yourself the gift of the pause. Any temporary discomfort will be eclipsed by the work you'll be able to sustain and the amazing change you'll be able to create in the world.

ACTION AND ORCHESTRATION TOOLBOX

☐ **Create prioritization lists.** Be intentional about what you're doing (and not doing right now) and track it visually in some way. You aren't tied down to those lists, but they serve as record-keeping and goal-setting that help you stay focused on the big picture.

☐ **Practice regular reflection.** The feedback that we get after taking action sets off the iteration cycle that hones the vision and inspires more action—as well as pointing to ways that you as a person fit into that vision. As you move through the Catalyst Formula, note what was intended, what happened, and how your energy levels responded along the way.

☐ **Get it on your calendar.** Magical thinking about what we can or should do in a certain time period skews us toward burnout. Get your priorities on your calendar, become mindful about the progress you're making and the time it takes, and use those reflections to adjust your priorities.

☐ **Create a Network Map.** Identify the context you're in and the players within it. Who could endorse you or influence the decision makers, and who might stand in your way? Where can you build influence that will expand or optimize that network?

- ☐ **Overcommunicate.** This is a practice in empathy and kindness that shepherds people through change in a way that they can embrace.
- ☐ **Breadcrumb.** Share information with your team in a way that empowers them to follow you and track the change back to you once the wins are realized.
- ☐ **Create space for change.** Free up your time by delegating wherever you're losing time and energy, pause to slow the process and re-ground with the formula, and proceed with a level of empathy that gives people permission to be uncomfortable, messy, and resistant.

CHAPTER 6

OPTIMIZING ITERATION

When John became the Director of Customer Engagement for Customer Programs at EMC, he brought all of his catalytic problem-solving skills—including a background in teaching and rural and regional development—with him. For example, while salespeople were trying to sell storage arrays, John could see the customers had a range of problems unrelated to storage. He cut a deal with the salespeople: *let us build a relationship with the customer and explore their problems, and I guarantee we'll sell your widget.*

John didn't set out to create something new. He just wanted to answer customer questions better.

John ran the Executive Briefing Center, and his team of four had a metric of five hundred customer "Show and Tells" a year. It was a clearly unfeasible metric that left them unable to create maximum impact, so John became curious about how he could shift that dynamic and explored what the most meaningful outcomes could be.

"The metric is beyond my ability to deliver as it stands," he told his boss. "Trust that we'll get you the results you need, but it can't be through a Show and Tell anymore." As you see in many successful Catalyst stories, John had a very supportive boss who listened, trusted, and ultimately gave him the freedom (and constraints) that he needed to thrive. The department was still given a mandate and a metric, but they also had freedom to figure out *how* to make it happen.

In the initial Show and Tells, customers would come in to be shown and told, a very traditional Executive Briefing Center approach. But then they would ask questions or share problems that he and his team couldn't answer. John wanted to understand why, so he started to explore in more depth. When customers pointed to offerings other ecosystem partners like Cisco and VMware were deploying, he got curious about whether those things could come together for EMC's business units and customers. He started asking internal stakeholders questions like, "What would happen if we put all of these components together?"

He began inviting those partners into the rooms for the customer meetings, which had by this point pivoted from a Show and Tell to true customer discovery, design thinking sessions. John then pivoted the process again by asking the engineering solutions group to prototype some examples of combined solutions. It became apparent that having technology assets come together to build a technical solution was one thing. They also needed to understand the business case they were validating. Each time he followed his curiosity, each time he pivoted to meet the customer needs, he built more momentum.

Department to department, across all three organizations, John helped to establish a small collaborative team to combine existing technology, services, and solutions into prototypes that better served customers and created more wins for everyone involved. Instead of setting up hundreds of "Show and Tells," they set up "Event Weeks," staffed by experts from the three companies. They could listen to many more customers over the course of the week, generating many more data points. They were able to sense trends in customer questions. "You actually accelerate the ability to move data between locations?" (Given this was pre-cloud, this was a Big Idea.)

John felt fortunate to have a boss who supported his iterative instincts and a team who all held catalytic tendencies. Instead of having to deliver five hundred individual meetings, John and his team were able to more deeply engage the entire ecosystem—internal teams, customers, and partners—to develop a groundbreaking offering. The solution became known as VCE, the virtual computing environment for VMware, Cisco, and EMC. Within a few years, it had snowballed out into its own $2.5 billion company and a whole new market category: converged infrastructure.

John credits the success of this initiative, in part, to the "go do" culture of the organizations involved. Because of the quick connections they made and rapid transitions from technology to business, they were able to take the Show and Tells off the table. All they had to do was provide the stage for the events. Then the trends, experts, existing technology, and potential intersections were clear, and salespeople who leaned into the process took it to the next level.

His curiosity around the data was rocket fuel to a culture willing to iterate. Rather than pitching a story to a customer, he would ask customers questions and show them how all of their threads came together. When they followed up on issues that challenged his narrative, ego didn't hold him back. Where he didn't know the answer, he'd find the person who did. He pushed for solutions outside of what they intended to provide.

Salespeople who followed John's methodology were better at upselling and cross-sales than before. And even when executives didn't completely buy in—one even flew out to rap them on the hands for their methodology—the bottom line spoke for itself. What can you say to a $12 million contract or a $2.5 billion spin out?

No undertaking is without its struggles or lessons learned, but John's story is one of unlocked potential. When Catalysts are free to make connections, to follow their curiosity, and to make adjustments to the plan, everyone benefits.

SUPERPOWERS AND BLIND SPOTS

Catalysts love movement. The moment we step into motion, we begin a loop of iteration that gives us even more data to puzzle out a solution. That data-collecting super ability of ours kicks in as we gather feedback that informs the next step, and the one after that. We take in the feedback that we generated, reflect on it, and update the vision and next steps accordingly. Sometimes, it affirms the path we're on, and sometimes, it sends us in a completely different direction. Either outcome is welcome because both simply represent new data.

We're not wed to the initial concept we come up with, because we understand it's just one step on the path to change. We're comfortable iterating because we're working in service of the higher vision, not our ability to be right the first time.

When something isn't successful, it simply points to where we can change.

However, if we're still operating from a state of unconscious competence, it's difficult to optimize our natural tendencies to lean into that tenacity and resilience.

The same part of us that's willing to sacrifice ego for the good of the project will also sacrifice self-care to the detriment of the work. The part that's willing to iterate will spin out on resistance instead of on the goal itself. The part that steps out with an imperfect idea will be vulnerable to crushing responses to that imperfection. The part that's comfortable with failure will hold stories about resistance and failures deep inside until we burn all the way out.

We are absolutely resilient, persistent, determined, tenacious, and fearless.

And those strengths can get us in trouble if we aren't consciously, mindfully keeping them in check.

In this stage especially, connecting to your process becomes an invaluable layer of resilience. It allows you to move through iteration with all of the intensity you're inclined to, without spiraling so quickly around resistance. It creates another pause that makes room for mindfulness and helps you hold the line between who you are and what you're doing in the world. It holds empathy at the forefront, reminding you that the work is in service of others, and pausing to bring them into it.

Yes, we want you to work well—but to do that, you need to fail well, too. That's what iteration is really about.

PAUSE WITH SHANNON

Iteration is both a superpower and a blind spot. It took me years to realize how much I internally iterate. How fast I iterate. How intuitively I iterate...without bringing other people on the journey.

My mind can move so fast, that on Monday I can agree with team members on the vision and their objectives, send them off to work on it—and by the time they come back to me with their completed work at the end of the week, I have a whole new vision of what we're working towards. Sometimes without even remembering that the first version existed.

Obviously, this is frustrating for everyone. In addition to the regular moments of reflection with my team and the priorities listed on my whiteboard, I've found a few other ways to at least minimize some of the impacts and frustration.

Counting the wins helps me and the team keep track of how much was accomplished when the vision has iterated (either intentionally or unintentionally). With one team offsite towards the end of the year, I had the team create sticky notes of everything we had accomplished. We started off and had a fair number of wins on the wall, only to realize we had only really gone back about six months. When we started to capture all of the things that we had done the first half of the year—the wall was covered—and our minds were blown. We had done so much. But because the vision had been constantly iterating, we had forgotten so many of the foundational things we had had to do to even create the vision and create the space we needed to start executing.

Building on that, I'm a big believer in the importance of celebrating those successes with the team. This is incredibly important both within your own direct team as well as with the wider stakeholder groups you're working with, whether it's a monthly spotlight or a more formal reward process. Being part of a change team is hard, and reminding people about what they've been able to accomplish is important. It's puts energy not just into that one person but the whole team.

I also have made sure to routinely leverage existing corporate rewards tools. It's a fantastic way to build momentum across the organization for your movement. They say that a movement only takes the second person to stand up and start singing with you. So recognizing all the supporters across the organization as they lean in to your work is not only the right thing to do but can help gain momentum. In every company I've worked for, there are corporate tools that help to amplify the person you are rewarding in a public venue across the organization. Help them shine! Give them the kudos! But make them meaningful and sincere.

Obviously, nothing speaks more highly of a contributor or collaborator's support than recognition from the top. If there's a CEO award program, leverage that. Nothing says "Thank you" better than a nod from the top usually combined with a significant financial reward as well. Not only do your supporters get their well-earned recognition and reward, but your program gets tied to that executive support. It's a win for all involved—a massive positive upward spiral.

While celebrating success, I have also long been a champion celebrating failures. Done in the right way, celebrating failures allows people the freedom to take calculated risks. When we learned that one of our hypotheses being tested by prototyping had reached a dead end, we killed the project with a party. We were clear on what we had learned and why it was better to stop before spending more money or time pursuing that line of inquiry.

I shared many of my own failures and lessons learned because I believe it's a great way to establish psychological safety. In retrospect, I wish I had celebrated more of the team's risk taking. It's a great way to demonstrate that not only will there be no retaliation for taking risks to try something new, you may actually be rewarded both for having the courage and having brought new learnings to the team.

TOOLS TO SUPPORT ITERATION

Iteration is meant to bring more clarity around our objectives and how we might manifest them. If we're dragging people into a cycle of failure when they aren't prepared, or glossing over their concerns instead of listening, or plowing through the next step and the next without any pause for celebration— if we're adding to the noise, we're doing everyone a disservice, including the work itself.

Recently, we developed our first line of courses within Catalyst Constellations. After a flurry of activity developing the structure and outlining the content, we reached out to people in the community for feedback and to let them know what we were doing. At the end of the weekend, we reflected:

Had we shared too soon?

Had we added noise that would just confuse our people later on?

In our excitement to help others work well, had we tripped up on some of the most basic things we advise others not to do?

Because we had our network mapped out from the beginning, we had our answers. We had been able to take those rough sketches and early models to just the right people. We knew who could handle ambiguity and who could be honest with us at that stage. With more data and further iterations, we had models that could go to the next level of people. It was that level of connection to a supportive network that allowed us to move something big forward quickly without it crumbling in our hands.

That doesn't mean we never fall into the traps that hold Catalysts back. But moving through the process with intention gives us a foothold where we'd otherwise create quicksand. Here are some of the tools we use to do so.

PRACTICE REFLECTION AND MINDFULNESS

While Mindfulness is by definition a rejuvenation practice, iteration is a reflection point that has to begin with this level of awareness. When we create space to work well, part of that space should be devoted to reflecting and making your iterative steps more mindful. Reflection is how to make your next steps a response rather than a reaction.

Mindful iteration looks at the vision you've articulated and asks what feedback you might need to make it clearer. It's the safe feedback and black hat questioning. It's going on Listening and Co-Creation Tours to gather more information and apply it to next steps.

Mindful iteration considers the action you've taken, what results came from it, and how you might need to adapt. It's the list-making and reflection that grounds magical, time-bending thinking back into reality. It's being truly empathetic as you listen to the people involved and discover what would make a win for them.

Mindful iteration is what keeps us from spinning out on resistance as quickly. When we get negative feedback and we instinctively want to scrap everything and start over or quit, pausing to reorient to the present moment and stage of the process can help us take more intentional steps.

Most of the time, our instincts are good. We're not going to sell Catalysts short there. Often, we can find success with an intuitive process that moves at lightning speed. But there's a cost to it, and pausing to bring more intention into your work will help mitigate that cost and make the payoff that much better.

REFRAME FAILURE

Catalysts reframe challenge quickly in their subconscious use of the Catalyst Formula. They get some feedback that tells them something should be tweaked, and they take it in stride—either iterating the vision or the steps toward the vision.

However, even Catalysts can be stopped dead in their tracks when big challenges are thrown in our way. When it feels like failure instead of just a speed bump, the tune changes.

Externalizing the Catalyst Formula becomes a way to remind ourselves that even when we are down on the floor feeling like a failure, a fraud, an impostor—we give ourselves the time to feel the feels, then we pick ourselves up again. It reminds us that iteration is an important part of the process, and that quickly learning that something didn't work is an important part of the process to understanding what does. The moment of failure gives us critical information that can be used to help us find that next, small step, to restart the action loop.

Your powers of resilience can be transmitted to people around you when you externalize them and take the time to bring people into your re-frame.

PROTOTYPE AND PIVOT

It's easier for us to reframe failure than our non-catalytic teams and counterparts. Prototyping allows us to test our vision against stakeholder feedback, customer desire, technical viability, and financial/business metrics—fast and without a ton of investment. If done properly, some (or many) prototypes *should* "fail" at some point. VCs plan for a roughly 10 percent hit rate. When you're pushing the envelope, failure is *expected*. It's how you know what will work and what won't before committing a whole product organization to develop a solution. It's a type of failure that creates agility and speed.

In her previous roles, Shannon made the reframing explicit: We have a prototype in motion based on customer needs that could either be carried on all the way to product development without points of true validation or we can set up iterative tests to produce data about why we should or should not move forward. She had the team test different hypotheses at each stage, and they would have to demonstrate the lessons we learned from it before a next go/no-go decision could be made.

We can celebrate the fact that we know more about what we should or should not be building to solve our customer's needs. And when we've killed something, we can have a party to celebrate the fact that we had learned a ton and haven't wasted ongoing resources on a doomed project.

For Catalysts, the pivot is definitional to who we are. Iteration is inherent in our process, so much that we don't always know that it's happening. Pivoting from lessons learned, new data gained, new visions emerging is part of our natural process. When we aren't careful, our pivoting process can add to our coworkers' confusion. They were just onboard with where we were headed, and we pivoted again, leaving them to wonder about our clarity and competency, and probably causing them to take a few steps back from contributing towards the new end state.

When we add the important reflection time between action and iteration, when we take the time to show people *why* we are pivoting by sharing the data with them in a way that makes it crystal clear what needs to be tested next, we can minimize the frustration on all sides. Without it, our pivoting becomes a maelstrom of energy that causes more harm than good.

The rest of the tools here—empathy for our teams and an intentional practice of celebration—help us survive the pivots that would otherwise be viewed as failures. Our first step is to rename them consistently. A lesson learned is just as important as any victory.

COUNT THE WINS

We iterate so quickly away from the details of the initial vision that we don't always remember what we pitched to begin with. It's no surprise we struggle with breadcrumbing. Those constantly moving goalposts make it difficult to ever feel successful, much less to point to those successes or celebrate them. Every step of action, every iterative loop erases the previous success point and gives us something new to aim for. We never reach the goal line, by our own design.

Even when we set high goals, we reach them in an anticlimactic way, then move on before the goal is achieved, or hit the peak and realize it was only the foothills with so much more to go. Then sometimes our phantom goals sneak in as well, and our attention is spread all over the place without any way of gauging what's important, what's been done, and what's getting in the way.

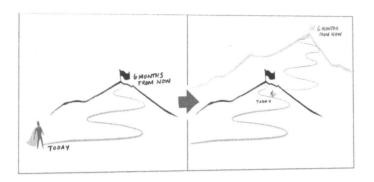

A practice of celebration—pausing to count the wins both for yourself and your team—facilitates the resilience, rest, and retention necessary to keep moving.

Yet this step is where our magical thinking turns dark and works against us. Once we find tools that we know are useful, we convince ourselves there's too much to get done to stop and use them.

This is little more than an excuse to keep us away from the uncomfortable work of prioritization, looking backward rather than forward or self-acknowledgement. Better a little discomfort now than the full burnout that awaits on the other end of this cycle. The longer we go without feeling successful, the harder we chase after phantom goals at the expense of our sleep and self-care, the more likely we are to lose our ability to work well. Do you want to keep going? Then pause and acknowledge where you've been.

CELEBRATE WITH YOUR TEAM

Feeling successful is an energy boost for everyone—Catalysts and non-Catalysts alike. The difference for us is that we're often working toward new modalities that literally haven't existed in the world before, or at least in our organizations. Often, the only goalposts are the ones we create. The only wins are the ones we acknowledge. If we want to share our energy and excitement for change with the people we're orchestrating that change with, we have to recognize the places where we've gained traction.

Celebration is a practice that can be as simple as an acknowledgment and as intentional as a scheduled reflection. We're going to look here at three key areas to celebrate with your co-conspirators:

- Regularly noting "gold star" moments
- Intentional reflection at plateau points
- Celebration with and from people outside of the team

As a regular occurrence, count the wins as often as you can. When you're reminded of your goal to celebrate more, stop and do it right then, especially if you feel like there's not enough time. Take five minutes and ask what went right in the last day, month, or year. Scribble the wins out onto notepads and white boards. Call out your successes toward the goal, including lessons learned that moved you forward. Utilize existing rewards structures and apply them to your wins.

When your celebrations call back to the first visual of your vision you set out with, the growth becomes that much more evident. One leader we worked with kept the original model for years, and she never stopped calling back to it. She could point to what eventually became seriously outdated and say, "Remember, this is where we started." Set a rhythm for those reflection points—every quarter, six months, or year—and look back before looking forward. Think about where you were vs. where you are now, giving credit where it's due for the progress made along the way.

Celebration outside of the team is just as important as within it. Sometimes, when an organization sees you as a Catalyst, whether or not they have a name for it, their magical thinking can be just as bad as your own. When you're still iterating after eighteen months and don't have an implemented product yet, it wears on people. Little wins are great, but whether or not you have something to show for it will eventually matter more. When you're not getting gold stars from the people looking over your shoulder, step outside of them. We're big believers in video as a powerful tool for communication—get your external and internal allies on record talking about what you've done. When your co-creators, each with their own credentials, can speak to the work as promising, innovative, and powerful, it becomes a source of encouragement and advocacy when others are beginning to fade.

Teaching your team to count wins outside of the final enacted product is more or less imparting your strengths as a Catalyst. People who aren't as energized by the feedback cycle as you are *need* to see just how much good is happening in the midst of what feels like spinning wheels. Rename the failures. Celebrate the pivots. Acknowledge the progress. Outside of the rejuvenation practices in the next chapter, this is one of the biggest energy-creators you can implement.

LEADING CHANGE: FEEDBACK TOURS

There is a cost to iteration, and we can inadvertently ask the people around us to pay it. When we bring the vision to other people, we have to consider the impact that change will have on them. We have to consider how comfortable they are with ambiguity and gray areas. We have to consider their agility in creative spaces and whether they'll be able to deliver feedback without being clouded by the feeling that their world is changing.

Iteration is stepping off the cliff toward the envisioned future on the other side, and not everyone is ready to go base jumping with us.

The Listening and Co-creation Tours that we've done to this point should open a door for feedback on fears, concerns, and resistance that our change might be creating in people around us as we shape the vision and drive toward action. Feedback Tours walk us back through the stakeholders and people who are affected by the change to make sure they feel heard and have buy-in on what is being shaped.

When we set out on a Feedback Tour, we are still open to the possibility that new data will change the action. But it happens late enough, after enough iterations, that it's more about them than us. We aren't packaging up our assumptions and dropping them in their laps but rather gathering up *their* assumptions and concerns about how the change will shape their world.

When we've stepped through the Catalyst Formula tools effectively, Feedback Tours also allow us to say things like, "Here's the vision that I built based on the conversations we had," or to point to the places where they were included.

Listening Tours and Co-Creation tours develop clarity and collective creativity on the change that's evolving, and Feedback Tours can generate more collaboration and buy-in as you enter later stages of the change.

Bringing this feedback into the iterative process keeps the change focused on people—in service to the bigger picture. It gives them a hand in the process, which will ultimately facilitate orchestration and create buy-in. It increases impact, knowing that you have co-conspirators ready to help you realize the thing you hope to manifest. And it holds us accountable to our breadcrumbing practice, so that we don't just allow the work to become invisible in a blur of unconscious iteration.

REJUVENATION TO OPTIMIZE ITERATION

Our rapid iterative process takes us from point A to B to D to Q before anyone knows what happened. The tools we've presented in this chapter ask us to acknowledge that blind spot. Our superpowers are most visible when we slow it down—not all the way to a halt but enough that we're not just a blur of action bouncing all over the organization.

We've already covered what that pause looks like: Articulate the vision. Make choices. Work in orchestration with others. Externalize the process. Teach others to share that same reframe around failure and tolerance for change. Mindfulness to be able to see your own iteration, to really see others' responses, to check your pace and communication, and to build processes and support relationships will all help you approach iteration without spiraling directly into burnout.

But if we're being completely honest here, you're probably going to hate pausing. It's going to feel incredibly, unnecessarily slow. That means you're going to need extra rejuvenation in this stage in order to sustain the work.

Empathy for others is always important, but don't let that eclipse compassion for yourself. Find people who will exhibit that same level of care and consideration toward you, who will understand where you're coming from and give you room to explore. Who will be brutally honest without being brutes. You need them, and chances are, they need you, too.

CONNECT TO OTHER CATALYSTS

John's biggest feedback for Catalysts is to find a community—and *community* is a small and inadequate word for what Catalysts actually create. The Catalysts in his team supercharged their ability to iterate, and feeling seen and supported allowed him to thrive personally as well as professionally. Finding people who deeply relate to you, who share your context and speak your language, is an experience that can't be distilled into one word and can't be replaced. As Catalysts, we need community to survive.

Specifically in iteration, having other Catalysts by your side is a game changer. Because everyone around John was actively working on the change and supportive of his work—because he was free to iterate toward the vision rather than getting lost in resistance—their Catalyst community was able to create a $2.5 billion spinout and change the face of his industry.

If you're not already part of a Catalyst community, a peer advisory group, or being coached by a Catalyst, it's time to make that happen. Emotional and psychological safety are key support tools for Catalysts who work well, and we can't always manifest those environments. Yes, this is a call to action to work with us, but it's bigger than that. There's a reason we offer the specific services that we do: Having a closed group or trusted advisor who knows you but isn't affected by your work is automatic spaciousness.

Yes, you might have to pause more than you'd like. The change might not happen as fast as everyone dreamed it could when magical-you came on board. But real, actual time-bending magic happens when you slow down enough to bring people along, and then the change actually does happen more efficiently because of it.

Rejuvenation slows the pace. Burnout grinds it to a screeching halt.

CELEBRATE FOR YOURSELF

"I don't care if I get credit for it. I just want it to exist in the world."

It's a noble thought that we all have, but it's largely unsustainable. Especially when "existing in the world" requires a lot of one-way, energy-draining work, or when we can't help but create the world we most want to see.

It's true that, when we reach the point where the idea is so integrated that people begin to think it was there all along, we've more or less won. The change has been made, the idea-baby is born, and we are free to move on to the next thing. If we've breadcrumbed well, there will even be a clear line between the change and our efforts. But the resume and company trust aren't all we're after. We have to follow the breadcrumbs, too, and acknowledge the win for our own confidence and credibility.

This is an uncomfortable necessity for most Catalysts. We're rarely in it for the fame and glory. We're just trying to satiate the burning sense that something needs to exist in the world. Seeking credit feels antithetical to who we are and how we work.

We often have to go for a long time without any credit to fully understand that counting wins is not about fame but validation. Yes, we want to see our work come to life, but we also want to be seen for who we are and what we're doing along the way. Fame is about credit for credit's sake—validation is about affirming our role and empowering it in the future.

We can get stuck—truly stuck—when we constantly have to prove our impact. The closer we are to the work, the more it can feel like proving our personal worth. The more invisible our impact, the more invisible we become. The parts of our process that cause discomfort or frustration are on full display, while the positive change is quietly absorbed into the process and culture.

So, celebrate.

Remind yourself of the good you've done. Mark what's happened along the journey, both to celebrate it and to remind yourself it's not magic. That might look like a reflection on your list at the end of the day, though another task can be easy to push away. If you can't make yourself pause daily, then choose another scale and stay accountable to it.

Like any other routine, we're most accountable to it when it's on our calendar—even better if someone is doing it with us. So schedule some time to celebrate. Set a meeting with yourself, blocked off so no one else can take it, and celebrate. Even if it has to be a celebration of the progress made toward your ideas, acknowledge your role in that work.

It'll help you articulate your value the next time you're asked. It'll re-energize you for the next phase of the work. And honestly, it just feels good. The world might need to be a better place, but you don't have to earn that role through self-aggrandizing and sacrifice. You are worthy of moments that feel good, too.

ITERATION TOOLBOX

- ☐ **Practice Mindful Reflection.** Iteration can be a danger zone for Catalysts, tempting us to spin out on the wrong things. Reflection and mindfulness, coupled with a routine of rejuvenation (next chapter), will sustain your energy through even the more difficult iterative processes.
- ☐ **Reframe failure**. Failing is a necessary and beneficial part of any work process that creates more data for us to work with. Embrace it for yourself and for the people you work with.
- ☐ **Prototype and pivot.** The vision and Action Map are going to change— if you're prototyping properly, something failing is actually a great sign. But it requires reflection, communication, empathy, and celebration for your team to move through this process without wearing them down.
- ☐ **Count the wins.** We tend to move the goal post the second a win is achieved, so that we never actually feel like we've won. Acknowl-

edge each success and failure, both personally and as a team or organization.

☐ **Connect with a community**. Important for every step of the Catalyst's journey, community gives us a place to reflect, pivot, commiserate, fail, grow, and celebrate where we are deeply seen and appreciated for who we are.

☐ **Celebrate.** Celebrate within your organization and outside of it. Celebrate for yourself and the people you work with. This isn't about ego or fame but about validation. And that will power your next efforts.

☐ **Go on a Feedback Tour.** Revisiting the people that you listened to in the beginning to catch them up on the vision and plan of action, get their stamp of approval, adjust any final major concerns, and earn their buy-in.

CHAPTER 7

WHOLE-SELF REJUVENATION

 When asked for an example of catalytic impact, Donna takes a step backward to clarify what impact actually is. "The kind of transformation that shows up as impact on the world requires lots and lots of small moments," she explains. "Persistence to drive a change, believing in that change, and showing up for it is what matters—not a single peak moment of impact."

Whatever change we create isn't a singular action at all, but the culmination of a lot of effort sustained over time. The tools we've delineated can make that effort more intentional and effective, but that doesn't remove the strain that we're putting our bodies and brains under throughout the process.

There is no single moment of change, and there is no end point to the changes we're inclined to make. The same connections, speed, and change that contribute to massive evolutions of organizations and culture are part of our everyday movement through life. The reverberations of our work surround us and leave that wake of chaos, victory, or a combination of both behind us.

Donna's deep understanding of this truth made her stand out amongst the other Catalysts in our early research. She was one of the few who had very little indication of burnout in her responses. She traveled, she worked hard, and she made incredible things happen—but her rejuvenation practices were so integral to her life that her energy sustained through it all. She didn't see herself as just a vehicle for change—she was her whole, amazing self, making catalytic change in the world. Her focus on routine and purpose has not only sustained but driven her career choices and successes.

Donna was the Vice President of Workspace Futures at Steelcase, during a massive effort to shift from market control to customer-centric practices. From the time that she and her team knew the shift was coming to the realization of breakthroughs she was driving toward, it took years of battling resistance and orchestrating change. The executives looking over her shoulder didn't always see the value of shoulder-to-shoulder work, constant coaching, or trust-building efforts, until an eight-week sprint helped bring the potential to life. Held over a summer and co-led by Donna and the new Head of Product Marketing, they introduced a structural shift in the way the company made choices, infusing design thinking and user experience insights to create better products for customers.

Out of those eight weeks, twenty actionable product solution sets were developed, then five were prioritized and fully funded. Because the organization had never looked at product development in that way before, there were no KPIs or comparisons to measure success, but hitting that 25 percent funding rate felt like a win to Donna and her team.

Coming into that role, Donna expected to be able to set out a path and watch the organization step through it. In fact, she chose that organization very specifically because they were so aligned to her values and purpose. She had been successful in previous roles, but being able to live in her dream location out in the middle of nature, for a company that prioritized care of the whole person, made Steelcase a perfect fit.

Even within alignment, however, we can find ourselves devoting a lot of personal time to role execution and hands-on work that we haven't accounted for. Donna recalls, "I had to devote a lot more of my own time to it than I ever expected...I assumed I could just say, 'Let's do it this way,' and then they would just lead it. When I realized they didn't know *how* to do it, I had to step in and execute a role I hadn't expected to." She reminds Catalysts that we have to commit to being in the vision 100 percent, even when that means giving up other parts of our jobs and expectations to do so.

Looking back, Donna believes that conscious planning for that expenditure of time and energy could have made the work more effective. What she was clear on from the beginning, however, was the importance of her rejuvenation practices. She stepped out for thirty-minute snowshoes during forty-five-minute breaks, found yoga studios to attend while traveling, and took brain breaks with her team. Donna's insistence on keeping her routines made her stand out from all the other Catalysts in early interviews. Burnout hadn't gotten to her in the way that others experienced.

To Catalysts who already feel bogged down in their work, she has an encouraging message: "Work is not all of life. Maintain that perspective. The more clear and intentional you are about the choices you make in your life, the more grounded you become."

PAUSE WITH SHANNON

I know the gig is up when this starts happening to me: The moment of resistance shifts into trauma. It feels like I am the lightning rod for the organization's resistance to pushing the change any further. By that point, I've turned myself into a source of energy for everyone else, with no way to recharge. It's just me and the work, trying to pull everyone along as best I can.

Each time this has happened—and it's happened every time—what I really lost was *distance*.

I get invited in to create change. The first early stages of change are incremental and successful. I gain trust and leeway to continue to pursue new types of change. I start seeing even bigger, better, bolder visions, and I get lost in the mania.

I move fast, I push the team hard, and as I move into orchestration, I start to see the next systems, processes, tools that need to be transformed in order to fully realize the next bigger vision. The bigger the change, the more the resistance starts to come, perhaps slowly at first but with increasing intensity.

At some point in the mania, I stop meditating and lose a bit of my mindfulness and rejuvenation practices. In the heady early days igniting the organization, I get my energy from the work. The successful new processes, products, customer contracts—the accolades and progress keep me going with a sense that I don't need to go to the gym today, a few more hours at work will be worth it.

But as the resistance mounts, the work doesn't give me the same energy. It starts draining more than it returns, and the work necessary to overcome resistance begins to feel like it's keeping me from the real work.

Burnout looks like twenty-seven migraines in thirty days. It looks like my body shutting down to the point that we were testing for critical diseases. It looks like no desire for any kind of rejuvenation practice, and no motivation for those practices even if I wanted them. It looks like not being able to get a good night's sleep for weeks on end.

As the resistance mounts in the organization, it's hard for me not to internalize it. When there is a lack of support for the hard work I am doing and when the environment doesn't provide a psychologically safe place for me to discuss how I'm feeling or how to make it better, I can internalize it even further. My negative self-talk track gets loud, taking away any last reserves of positive energy I started with, ending up with discouragement and self-doubt.

I have figured out over the years a few ways to slow down the cycle even as I struggle to avoid it completely.

I know now that what happens along this work cycle is largely unconscious. I keep pushing further and harder, not because I want to sacrifice anything for the work, but because that magnetic pull of a challenge speaks to the core of my being. Having that knowledge isn't going to keep me from ever dipping toward burnout again, but I don't have to struggle alone, and I don't have to run my body into the ground. The more conscious I become of that magnetism, the more aware I am of my strengths and protective of what makes those strengths sustainable. More importantly, I'm more likely to see change through to my desired end.

The realization of the need for self-compassion as an antidote to internalizing resistance to change came when I attended Peter Senge and

Otto Scharmer's Executive Champions Workshop. That experience gave me so much clarity about how I had lost myself and what I needed to do to rebuild—I needed to focus on self-compassion. Being surrounded by a group of self-aware, compassionate humans who held beautiful space for me was incredibly healing. But I knew it was just the beginning. I have since taken a Mindful Self-Compassion class twice. It has helped me develop a regular practice that helps keep me sustained and maintain a spaciousness between me and my work.

As a founding principle of Catalyst Constellations, Tracey and I have built awareness of these essential tools into our business practices, including rejuvenation in our partner meetings, starting each session with a moment of mindfulness with all our group gatherings, and supporting each other through our own energetic curves. Finding environments that support mindfulness and our whole selves is an amazing gift for Catalysts, at every point on the energy curve.

THE SUPERPOWERS ARE THE BLIND SPOT

Most of us fall more toward Shannon's experience than Donna's—it's rare to have innate superpowers around rejuvenation, and the powers that we do have require us to develop rejuvenation practices that much more. Our commitment to action and impact is often the very thing that undoes us.

When we set out to manifest change, the passion that we bring to the table can be magnetic. We're the new shiny thing, carrying vision and potential all wound up in an energetic ball of hope that it will come to life. But when resistors, stakeholders, or even the person who brought us in isn't actually ready for change, that magnetic field is reversed. What once drew others in becomes a repellant—scary, dangerous, exhausting, and impossible. We pull them quickly into new ideas and ways of being that they aren't quite ready to adopt, still hopeful that manifestation is possible. Still in motion despite the resistance we're pulling against. We're still hopeful for change, though our balloon of space is now pulled so tight that we're the ones beginning to snap.

In worst-case scenarios, the combination of our energy for change, a lack of distance between ourselves and the work, and the organization's resistance to change turns to trauma. We feel gaslit up to a breaking point, then when we snap it "proves" that we're volatile. We get worn down by verbal abuse until we begin to believe the bullshit. Our dynamic thinking and creativity begins to crumble as psychological safety, care for our whole selves, and energy erodes.

The superpowers that we love about ourselves can power our downfall, and all while we hold the best of intentions. In other words, burnout isn't just an experience of physical exhaustion or a result of working too much. It's the end of a physical, emotional, and cognitive battle that we couldn't win within a war that we can't help but fight.

Rejuvenation is a small word for what we're creating with these tools. It's the antidote to the trauma and burnout that frequently comes with the long process of change that we continuously engage in.

Naming trauma and burnout directly gives us the power to address it, to get around those reactive responses and return to a level of creativity. Reclaiming a place of psychological safety and rediscovering a sense of purpose allows us to work creatively in spite of the struggle that we're buried under. And when we hold a routine that prioritizes physical, emotional, and cognitive rejuvenation, we gain the space necessary to pause and respond in spite of the way our brains and bodies want to react to trauma.

This is the key to working well, Catalyst. It's how we pay the invoice that our magic hands to us. It's not going to be easy— but if we're honest, that *could* be what we like about it.

DEFINING AND RECOGNIZING WORKPLACE TRAUMA: JENNIFER HARKNESS, MA, LMHC, ATR

Frequency of burnout is one of the strongest shared tendencies amongst Catalysts, often discussed in tandem with a sensation of "trauma." Colloquial phrases like corporate PTSD, traumatic history, and triggers all come up when we're talking about the experiences that helped pull us into burnout, and as it turns out, there is a fair amount of research to back up those connections. We spoke with trauma specialist Jennifer Harkness about what trauma is and how it affects us, especially in the workplace.

First, Jenn is quick to separate the experience of trauma from the clinical expression of PTSD. While the latter has diagnostic thresholds and requires serious care, trauma itself exists on a spectrum of personal experience. Not everyone who experiences trauma will develop PTSD, and if two people live through similar experiences one may register it as trauma and the other may not. "I've seen people register trauma when their parents didn't buy them fifty-dollar mascara, and I've seen people witness gruesome death without registering it as trauma. You can't tell a person what's traumatic."

Jenn suggests we consider trauma as a spectrum, where on one side you have interpersonal trauma and on the other side experiences like war and rape. Within that there are types: acute (one time), chronic (ongoing), and complex (ongoing and interpersonal, like an abusive home or toxic work environment). Jenn explains that psychologists are still in an early phase of understanding trauma. In recent history, for example, bullying was discredited as a source of trauma, where we now know it can be a significant factor. Bullies are in workplaces, not just on playgrounds.

Research in the area of workplace trauma is incipient, but the growing body supports the experiences that Catalysts talk about when experiencing passive aggressive behavior, shunning, ignoring, backstabbing, gossip, or criticism. This is emotional abuse. The rates of anxiety and depression are very high for people that have experienced workplace bullying.

Bullies aren't our only threat as Catalysts, either. We're often hired specifically to make change, without the organization knowing if they are actually ready for that change. "Resistance is not a problem," Jenn says. "It's actually showing us where we need to go. That kind of conflict is part of being creative with people—as long as there is psychological safety involved."

So what does it feel like to experience workplace trauma? Jenn tells us it's hardwired. Trauma is triggered by a feeling of threat to our basic needs, and in the workplace our livelihood is always on the line. When our jobs feel threatened by criticism, ostracizing, or even a passive aggressive sense of gaslighting, trauma response takes over. That's our natural instinct to fight, flight, freeze, or faint. None of those responses are conducive to productive, creative, clear, catalytic thinking.

There are a lot of factors of resiliency related to your biology as well, however, such as how your nervous system is wired to the support network that you have. Your community and workplace structures contribute to the way you cope with and assimilate trauma. A favorite quote of Jenn's comes from Peter Levine: "Trauma is hell on earth, but trauma resolved is a gift of the gods."

Post-traumatic growth and resiliency center around psychological safety. If we want top-notch teams and good performance in our organizations, Jenn notes that we *have* to have psychological safety. We have to get rid of fear tactics and stop incentivizing the toxic people and bullies who perpetuate workplace trauma.

This is not something individual Catalysts often have control over, so instead we must focus on our own healing and resilience.

The neurological response to trauma is to hijack our thinking and processing brain's ability to self-regulate, replacing it with the reactivity of the inner brain. The amygdala sends distress signals and activates an adrenaline response—fight, flight, freeze, or faint.

Identifying that loss of regulation and replacing it with intention can slow down the moment and bring our creativity back online. It's also important to identify, create, and protect our own areas of psychological safety.[15] That means looking for and cultivating spaces of active listening and communication. When our conflicts can be named and worked through, we get the most out of the messiness of creativity. When it turns into an interpersonal battle, or an environment of neglect and verbal abuse, that sense of safety is removed and trauma can result.

Jenn's a veteran of this work. She completed her master's thesis on vicarious trauma, compassion fatigue, and burnout, which highlights another important clarification around the relationship between trauma and burnout. That is, burnout is as complex as the trauma that leads to it.

---

15   Harvard's Amy Edmondson coined the term psychological safety. We recommend her book, *Teaming*, for more.

For people working in broken environments—first responders, health-care workers, and advocacy work in particular—the unsustainability of the work creates a kind of burnout called *moral injury*. In this scenario, we were never going to be able to avoid that burnout, because the system is set up to fail.

"I am a Catalyst, and I personally have experienced this," Jenn offers. "It's why I don't work in community mental health anymore." Jenn was experienced as being "too much" of an advocate for her clients. Her drive to create change and passion for her clients were so contrary to the system at the time that she went into private practice instead. Since then, she has noticed that things have changed, and she finds that healing. "Oftentimes, you look back and you see, 'I was onto something really important and that's why they hated it.' That is a common story I hear from employees, too. And that leads to post traumatic growth and resiliency."

That is to say, there are times when simply exiting the organization is an act of rejuvenation—when you have to let them continue the journey without you. Talking yourself into doing better and trying harder is tempting, as is often the case in any abusive situation. But if you're in an unsustainable environment within an unchangeable system, Jenn's advice is clear: "Leave." Cut ties, recover, and move on—being sure to pursue individual therapy and mindful self-compassion as you heal. A safer environment is waiting for you, your gifts, and the change you're destined to make.

THIS IS BURNOUT

When resistance or mutually inflicted trauma looks like a new challenge to tackle, we revert back to what we know. We need energy in that moment, and the last time we had it was in the early stages of a challenge. So we begin to try to solve the problem of the resistance with cycles of Vision, Action, Iteration. Unfortunately, we are often doing it while too close to the original problem. We might push our data as proof of the original vision rather than reading the people and room with empathy to discover the real source of the problem. This is especially difficult when people around us have determined that *we* are the problem. That our drive toward change, or at least our workstyle as we do so, is what needs to be fixed.

Any energy gained in this stage is false. Instead of climbing a mountain that will eventually have a beautiful summit to enjoy, we're digging a trench that will eventually feel impossible to escape.

Burnout looks like not wanting to get out of bed in the morning. It looks like being distracted, unfocused, unfulfilled, frustrated. It looks at work as if it is a battleground.

Burnout is a sense of disconnect from self, community, and the organization. It's working too hard and too fast without making enough progress in the right direction. It's an energy leak without any replenishment.

In the early days, we often explain those signs away:

- I'm just tired.
- It's just this project.
- It's just that person.
- After this, I'll sort it out.
- I'll get better, do better, be better, work better.

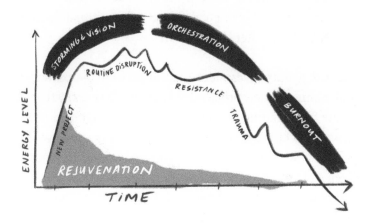

But when we dismiss the early warning signs, it eventually hits a point where we *can't* do better. Repeating cycles of interpersonal trauma consistently strains our neurological responses and diminishes our capacity to work. The longer we stay there, the more entrenched those patterns become, and the longer the work is delayed.

We've been clear from the beginning that there's no way to guarantee a life without burnout. But when we see the signs coming and decide to heed them, we can bottom out with less frequency and amplitude. We can turn to our rejuvenation practices (or cultivate new ones) to realign and get back to work.

BE AWARE OF YOUR ENERGY TANK

Donna's rejuvenation practices are the gold standard. They are why her story of a prolonged battle with resistance didn't end in dramatic burnout. If she hadn't seen herself as a whole person and prioritized the things that feed her physically, emotionally, and cognitively, she wouldn't be able to show up to create the incremental changes that ultimately led to the realization of her larger vision.

The path to burnout cannot be decoupled from the excitement and mania of a new project that we love. The energy that we create from finding new challenges and facing them masks how much energy it costs, and we overestimate how long we'll be able to sustain it. For example, working on minimal sleep and powering through without personal time feels fine early on, but we forget how hard that can be later on in the cycle. If we carry those habits into the next phases or begin to think of them as the norm, that energy return won't be able to compensate anymore, and burnout will result.

Our ability to protect rejuvenation practices at all stages of the journey and as part of all pieces of the Catalyst Formula determine our ability to carry out the work. But it does take energy and determination to create and protect a routine of rejuvenation, so before we can do that, we have to name the trauma and burnout that we've experienced or are actively struggling against.

For this key tool, we need to take off the blinders and gently bring our energy to consciousness. What is creating real energy, what masks as giving energy, and what is taking it away? A simple awareness of energy depletion will determine whether we can conserve and sustain it through the difficult, later stages of a project or manifestation.

ENERGY TANK

VACATION

MEDITATION

YOGA

WALKS

This doesn't have to become a prolonged daily exercise that takes your time—because it's a function of awareness, it can be done in the seams. During the workday, pay attention when certain meetings drain you, or certain people leave you exhausted. Pay attention when you procrastinate and dread doing certain tasks. Acknowledge the moments, people, and tasks that give you energy—when you're flying high after that moment and feeling great about your work.

Bring even more awareness to potential burnout and its antidote by writing down what activities give you energy and what activities deplete your energy. As a baseline, we want to see it balance out. The second we have more activities that take energy than give it back, we're in a danger zone for burnout. Period. No excuses, no rationale, no powering through.

Specifically, committing to a rejuvenation routine is less about doing the same thing over and over again, and more about consistently refilling your tank. If yoga, meditation, and self-compassion all give back, there should be time on your calendar and practices in your routine that make space for those things.

In some cases, these energy sources will be able to counter sources of potential burnout, refilling them faster than the slow leak takes it away. Be aware of the complete, one-way energy drain, however. If you're holding your routine and still finding yourself depleted and constantly near burnout, something significant will need to change.

QUESTIONS TO ASK YOURSELF TO ASSESS IF YOU ARE NEARING OR IN BURNOUT

The Mayo clinic points to these questions that can help us identify early warning signs of burnout:[16]

1. Have you become cynical or critical at work?
2. Do you drag yourself to work and have trouble getting started?
3. Have you become irritable or impatient with co-workers, customers, or clients?
4. Do you lack the energy to be consistently productive?
5. Do you find it hard to concentrate?
6. Do you lack satisfaction from your achievements?
7. Do you feel disillusioned about your job?
8. Are you using food, drugs, or alcohol to feel better or to simply not feel?
9. Have your sleep habits changed?
10. Are you troubled by unexplained headaches, stomach or bowel problems, or other physical complaints?

---

16   "Job Burnout: How to Spot It and Take Action," Mayo Clinic, last modified November 21, 2018, https://www.mayoclinic.org/healthy-lifestyle/adult-health/in-depth/burnout/art-20046642.

PRACTICE MINDFULNESS

As we just heard from Jenn, practicing mindfulness—especially mindful self-compassion—is one of the ways we can begin to heal from trauma and burnout. But these tools can support us no matter where we are in the Catalyst Journey, because let's face it, creating change is hard. And we can be incredibly hard on ourselves, without ever realizing we're doing it.

Across the Catalyst Journey, mindfulness becomes a muscle that we build by paying attention—intentionally, in the moment, and without judgment—to what's actively happening in, through, and around us. In chapter X, we pointed to the Catalyst Formula and how mindfulness brings that process to the forefront rather than it being a blur of unconscious intuition. Mindfulness helps Catalysts slow down to more effectively create change and minimize burnout, through:

- Mindful Self-Compassion
- Mindful Self-Awareness
- Mindful Empathy
- Mindful Intentionality

We often find that the earliest stages of mindfulness—just seeing that you are not alone in your catalytic experiences—helps Catalysts cut themselves some slack. It's *healing* to know you aren't alone. Maybe you were born this way, maybe you evolved into being this way, but it doesn't matter. At this point, it's *who you are*. And even more importantly, the world needs more of you.

We're finding new Catalysts and expanding the network every day, but while there are many different varieties of

Catalysts, there is also only one unique you, who sees the world as a brighter, better, healthier future. And that is a gift. This is why we're writing the book. To help you see yourself for who you really are, with all your incredible superpowers, and to bring those powers top of mind so that you can use them with intention.

We've also brought the blind spots to a state of mindfulness, so that you can see what nobody has told you before. That yes, you are flawed and have room to grow, but if you use these few tools to support your journey and work around some of your edges, you will be *unstoppable*.

MINDFUL SELF-COMPASSION

We've been told our whole lives we're different (at best) and disruptors, troublemakers, and pains in the ass (at worst). But it's who we are. We can't help that we're fast and driven by a deep need to make everything better. So, little by little, we internalize the external voices. "She's too much." "He's too intense." "She should stay in her swim lane." "Who do they think they are?" And that nasty little internal critic that most people have becomes unbearably loud for the Catalyst.

That drive we are born with to make things—well, *everything*—better, is exhausting. Even if we encountered very little resistance, there are just so many damn ways the world needs to be improved. We couldn't possibly get to them all. Which can make us feel badly about ourselves.

The more projects we don't see through to the end—because who wants to dot the Is and cross the Ts?—the less "credibility" we have on our resumes. Of course, those myriad new things wouldn't exist in the world without us launching them. But if we didn't take the time to breadcrumb the impact back to us, organizations have a hard time articulating our value.

Frankly, *we* have a hard time articulating our value.

We internalize the label of troublemaker and look back to see a long history of what the world considers "half-finished" projects, and we tell ourselves we suck. We're imposters. Masters of nothing.

The only way out of this mindset is self-compassion. And no one can do this for you but you.

Self-compassion is a scientifically validated antidote to these stories. And mindfulness is a key component of reversing the negative talk track—paying attention when that voice arises and changing the narrative.[17]

MSC comes from Kristen Neff's research and practice on combining traditional mindfulness practices (meditation, gratitude practices, loving kindness, etc.) to facilitate self-awareness, self-acceptance, and self-forgiveness—all ultimately supported by self-compassion.

The core of self-compassion consists of three pillars:

1. Mindfulness—being present with non-judgment
2. Loving Kindness—tenderness and consideration

---

17   Loving kindness towards ourselves and an understanding of our common human shared experience are important here, too. Kristen Neff and Christopher Germer discuss this in *The Mindful Self-Compassion*.

3. Common Humanity—a sense of interconnectedness and shared experience with all beings

Each of these individual pillars can help us on its own, and the collective impact of the three helps us to find compassion for ourselves. It helps us gain clarity about ourselves and the situations we find ourselves in. MSC can help us create the necessary distance between ourselves and the work. It creates a solid foundation of resiliency.

Some common questions in MSC help us reframe how we treat ourselves vs, how we would treat others: "How would you treat a friend in this situation? What would you say to them? What tone of voice would you use? What would you say to comfort them?"

With this perspective of mindful self-compassion as our base of strength, we come to learn and accept that we are just doing our best, while still being committed to constantly improve. We learn to forgive ourselves for mistakes with grace and confidence, which allows us to model that comfort with failure for others. It gives us our own unique power and confidence to stand in, which helps us keep external criticism at bay. When our boss or the organization starts attacking us and then our ideas, it becomes a shield that can protect us from some of the worst of it seeping in. And it helps give us the strength to know when to walk away.

And it doesn't mean that we don't listen to the feedback entirely when it's given. We do make mistakes. People can share their feedback, bosses can evaluate, and partners can criticize. It does mean that we have the skills to deeply sense which part of the feedback resonates, own it, authentically apologize when appropriate, make adjustments, and *move on*. It frees us from ruminating on it more, even after we've apologized ten times profusely. It gives us the space to more productively make changes and freely jump into the next thing we're going to make better.

By bringing all these things to consciousness, we can more readily (though rarely easily) forgive ourselves. By developing self-compassion, we can create a distance between ourselves and the critiques that are being lobbed at us. We can see the negative feedback for what it is, make changes when we choose to, and more easily let the unhelpful attacks roll-off our backs. It's not that we won't heed some critical feedback, but we will do so as a choice, and without letting it compromise our sense of self-worth—or at least as much.

Even the most experienced MSC practitioners get their feelings hurt. It doesn't make us impervious to criticism or bullying. But it helps us gain the clarity faster. It helps us contextualize more quickly. And it helps us get up off the floor, dust ourselves off, and begin the search for the next big challenge where we will be more supported and valued. This gives us the freedom to also choose to walk away when an environment is just too toxic.

Forgive those people, too, but start with yourself.

You deserve it.

You've been doing your best. If you never realize all the change you want to see, big or small, that's ok. The only one really keeping track is you. So be kind. Give yourself a big hug. And know that it's not only ok, but it's *vital* that you put your own oxygen mask on first by being kind and compassionate to yourself.

Remember, we never promised that you could avoid burnout, but a strong mindful self-compassion practice can decrease the frequency and diminish the depths.

MINDFUL SELF-AWARENESS

Physiologically, mindfulness can become an early warning system for stress. There's a reason we describe so many gripping emotions with physical words "You're blowing my mind" or "His blood is boiling." Developing skills around noticing your heart rate increasing, feeling stress in your shoulders, or experiencing discomfort in the gut can in turn create better self-awareness of emotional states that we'd otherwise miss.

This can be a particularly helpful tool if we're swirling around in our heads, to help us notice with more clarity our emotional state.

Now put that understanding in the context of the Catalyst: When you are speaking with a co-worker is your heart rate elevated, are you going in ready to be defensive instead of coming in ready to listen? Are you in a triggered state with your body in a fight or flight mode because someone is attacking you or your idea? Is your physical system so run down that you know it's time for more rejuvenation?

Emotionally, practices of mindfulness that tune us in to self-awareness of our thought patterns and physical state make us better able to self-regulate our emotions. The earlier we interrupt a chain of negative associations the better. We can stay calmer, more centered, and less reactive. It can help us better self-regulate when we encounter situations that might start off by triggering us. We can actually start to choose to lean into different emotional states and let go of ones that aren't serving us.

For the Catalyst, consider whether you are in a state of mania and euphoria that indicates you may need to go back to your rejuvenation practice. Are you feeling frustrated with your team's pace? Are you feeling lonely and exhausted from the sense of pulling the entire organization forward? Are you at a point of burnout where something needs to materially change?

Finally, watching thoughts go by with detachment allows us to witness the cognitive patterns of our brain. For example, it allows us to notice whether we are worried about the future or spend time feeling regret or longing for the past. We can think of it as sitting on the bank of a river watching boats drift by—we can notice their color, their speed, their size, power, without desiring to get in them and sail away.

As a Catalyst, Mindfulness that supports self-awareness can help us gain more clarity. Are we clear on our vision or are we just bouncing from idea to idea? Are we holding onto phantom goals that we need to let go of? Is it time to inject some more reflection and pauses into our process to slow down the speed of thought and action?

MINDFUL EMPATHY

Research has also shown that in addition to helping to develop self-compassion, mindfulness—especially in the form of meditation—helps improve compassion towards others, starting with empathy.

If we can attune more subtly to what we're feeling, we can also attune to what others are feeling. By slowing down our reactivity, by being able to witness our own reactions to a given moment, we can also cultivate the ability to develop sensitivity to other people's experiences—which cultivates a sense of empathy. As we've already seen, empathy can help us as we move through the change process to ensure that we're bringing people along in a productive way.

As Catalysts, we move fast. We can leave others behind. Even when others want to support the vision, they may not always know how.

Bringing empathy into your work through a practice of mindfulness allows you to slow down and bring others along more effectively. It helps you be more understanding of different (and most likely slower) abilities to deal with change.

It cannot be said enough: bringing empathy into your relationships as you create change makes you a more effective Catalyst.

MINDFUL INTENTIONALITY AND PACING

Mindfulness brings the Catalyst Formula to the forefront by helping us slow down to take important pauses. Those moments of pause create space to more clearly evaluate the current situation for what it is, without imposing our view or will onto the situation. From there, it creates clarity for our next steps.

This doesn't mean we'll stop moving fast. But at full speed, sometimes we unintentionally break shit. Without self-awareness and intentionality, we often burnout hard.

Without pausing to bring this process to consciousness over and over again, we can lose ourselves and others in our speed to make the world a better place. Even the most adept and senior Catalysts can get caught up in the thrill and forget to pause, reflect, and reconnect with the Catalyst Formula.

By building time into our rejuvenation practices for stillness, we can give ourselves the opportunity to pause, witness our thoughts more clearly, and cultivate a considered non-reactive response. From there, we can go back to the Catalyst Formula, and make stronger, more intentional choices for the most effective next steps.

Mindfulness is a process through which we all can become more present and self-aware. It allows us to leverage the Catalyst Formula with more intentionality. We become more effective Catalysts, while minimizing burnout and sustaining our ability to continue doing amazing things in our respective worlds.

ESTABLISH PSYCHOLOGICAL SAFETY

The concept of psychological safety was first explored in the 1960s by organizational scholars and regained popularity in the 1990s. According to organizational behavior scientist Amy Edmondson, it's "a shared belief held by members of a team that the team is safe for interpersonal risk taking."[18] In Google's

---

18   Amy Edmondson, "Psychological Safety and Learning Behavior in Work Themes," *Administrative Science Quarterly* 44, no. 2 (June 1999): 350-383, https://doi.org/10.2307/2666999.

more recent exploration about the characteristics of high performance teams, psychological safety is number one on their list.[19] Google defines it as "team members feel safe to take risks and be vulnerable in front of each other." One of the world's top innovative and most valuable companies stresses the importance of psychological safety. If we had to bet, there's a fair few Catalysts at Google—we've worked with some of them. And while psychological safety is important for all teams, it's particularly important when your actual job responsibilities include taking risks to create change. It's crucial for Catalysts.

Psychological safety is a two-way street. Without the tools we've worked through in previous chapters—practices that help us slow down, create empathy, and ease them through the change—the people around us can feel just as unheard as we feel unsupported. The less distance we have between the progress and ourselves, the more likely we are to interpret resistance and conflict as threats to our safety. Sometimes we are even directly told we are the problem, even as we're making progress in the change we've been brought into create. But remember that trauma is a hardwired response to a threat—and sometimes we are the threat. That means we can inflict as much trauma as we experience.

As a catalytic leader, creating a culture of psychological safety may be one of the most important skills you can develop. If you expect your team to step out on a limb to provide divergent thinking, you need to let them know they're safe. If a difficult conversation arises when considering different options, people need to know that there won't be retaliation later. People need to be able to ask for help when they need

---

19   "re:Work," Google, https://rework.withgoogle.com/print/guides/5721312655835136.

it without fear of being perceived as weak or incompetent. If you're asking a team to iterate all the time—and if you've pivoted from "failure" to recognizing the new data as learning—the team needs to feel confident that this pivot will be translated to leadership levels as well.

We all know what it feels like when a team doesn't have this trait as a core value, and we've already discussed bullying, which is the antithesis to psychological safety. You've been asked to come up with new ways of doing things. You've done your homework. You've done a Listening Tour. You think you've got it all buttoned up.

But then you present your vision, and get completely shut down.

You hear all about what a bad idea it is, and by the end of the meeting, everyone has jumped on the bandwagon with resistors and your ideas are torn to shreds. That's not very motivating for the next time you're asked to present a few new solutions.

Psychological safety requires a leader to practice active listening and curiosity, authenticity, non-reactivity, a willingness to let go of perfectionism, patience, an ability to admit when we've made mistakes, encouraging collaboration, and a strong practice of celebrating wins. It means letting people stretch beyond their comfort zones and balancing motivational and constructive feedback.

This sounds like a long list, and it is! But this is where mindfulness becomes a great tool. It helps us develop the self-awareness to develop and strengthen all of these skills.

Imagine how this empowers your team: They know they can bring almost any new crazy idea to the team for consideration, because that's how new ideas are born. The team asks appreciative questions, you build on each other's ideas, people even lean in to help you with the next iteration or pivot. The team co-creates incredibly well, and there is a high level of trust. Maybe your idea doesn't get wings this time, but everyone on the team knows that you're undeterred and will be back with your next amazing idea soon. In fact, the team celebrates the person who brings the most new ideas, in addition to the person who brought the most ideas that made it through the process.

If you're not in a leadership position, you can certainly model these behaviors for your peers, colleagues, and even boss. But since you don't have direct control of the team culture, you have to evaluate for yourself how psychologically safe or unsafe you are. It's a scale, not binary. No manager is ever perfect in gracefully receiving all ideas and not all teams collaborate perfectly. But if you're feeling like it's unsafe, if people on the team are constantly berated, if it's starting to cause you trauma, it's time to pause and reflect. If you feel like it's better to just keep your head down then speak up, then it's time to evaluate your next move.

One of the most common questions we get when Catalysts start self-identifying, is how they can tell if their current team or potential new organization will be a safe and supportive place. To evaluate a team or leader's ability to create a psychologically safe environment, you can work with the questions posed by Edmondson:[20]

---

20 Amy Edmondson, "Team Learning and Psychological Safety Survey," in "Psychological Safety and Learning Behavior in Work Teams," *Administrative Science Quarterly* 44, no. 2 (June 1999): 350-383, doi:10.2307/2666999, https://www.midss.org/content/team-learning-and-psychological-safety-survey.

- If someone makes a mistake in this team, is it often held against him or her?
- In this team, is it easy to discuss difficult issues and problems?
- In this team, are people sometimes rejected for being different?
- Is it completely safe to take a risk on this team?
- Is it difficult to ask other members of this team for help?
- Do members of this team value and respect each other's contributions?

Keep in mind that every other tool that we have talked about in this book is something for you to cultivate and leverage personally. Psychological safety *has* to be established by the leader. And when it's not there, it's almost impossible to change as it requires a willingness to do deep personal work. A leader needs to feel confident enough in themselves to admit failure, while being comfortable enough with ambiguity to allow the team to explore new ideas and admit when they need help. Sadly, these aren't traits that have been historically celebrated as essential in leadership development. Though there is one silver lining to our VUCA reality—all of that is starting to change.

REVISIT EMPATHY AND THE NETWORK MAP

As much as we've presented Catalysts as the superhero, that doesn't automatically make our detractors villains. Someone who creates trauma isn't necessarily a bad person. In fact, we spent a fair amount of time discussing ways that we might trigger other people into fear and self-protection, which can inflict trauma on them as well. After all, we're all in this together, doing the best that we can as very different kinds of people.

The Network Map that we created and used in previous chapters is not just about the process of manifestation—it's about identifying and utilizing safety nets. It helps us share information with people who won't be quite so shaken by the thought of big change. It helps us turn to supporters to shield us when we feel like there's a target on our backs.

The Network Map becomes a tool of rejuvenation when we use it to identify places of safety—for us, our ideas, and our peers.

When co-workers or managers are creating what feels like an unsafe environment, it's often not their intention. It's easy to vilify them and make ourselves the well-intentioned victims, if we don't bring in empathy and try to understand what their world looks like. That boss who has completely removed their support from you might not have any space between themselves and the work either. Consider what their life is like—the weight, exhaustion, and burnout they might be feeling. Consider how most people and organizations are hardwired to reject the kind of change you're driven toward. Bring empathy into each interaction, not to shame yourself into carrying more weight but to shift the expectations you hold and create distance.

This mindfulness allows you to become an observer of the situation—you are seeing more complete interactions between yourself and the other person, complete with backstories. Your reactivity slows, giving you time to respond to what's actually happening rather than what it feels like. You see how they are reacting as well, to experiences long in their past rather than only to you. It helps you avoid getting caught up in the drama of the moment, because you're playing the long game.

And the Network Map reminds you the role each person and interaction plays in that game.

At the same time, you have to practice the same kind of reliability and compassion in our interactions with others that you would like to see from your leaders. Walk the talk. If someone raises their hand on an issue, listen deeply to them. Don't gloss over it or move quickly past it. Model the empathy that creates a safe space, and ideally that will have a knock-on effect throughout the organization. Be the psychologically safe place for your co-workers.

Rejuvenation practices create the container of mindfulness and awareness that support our natural process. It allows us to move through Vision, Action, and Iteration making grounded choices rather than spinning out in reactivity and a lack of awareness. What we gain from that intentionality is the confidence that past burnout and trauma took from us.

Now, there is a dividing line that exists somewhere in this plane of resistance that moves from the Catalyst's responsibility to work well with others and into the organization's responsibility to be psychologically safe. In his book *The Speed of Trust*, Stephen Covey simplifies trust to two traits: character and competence. The person you're engaging with on a vulnerable level should create space for psychological safety both in the team *and* their relationship with you. If they don't continually behave in ways that demonstrate trust, don't give it to them unmerited. At some point, no amount of fearlessness, confidence, or even empathy will break through those walls, and it will be time to move on.

RECONNECT WITH PURPOSE

Some Catalysts are clear on an aggregate lifetime Purpose—exactly what they're meant to do in this world. And that capital-P sense of Purpose drives their every step. Others simply find purpose in each job, each year, each moment. In both cases, holding a strong sense of purpose creates energy that sustains us and keeps us focused.

There's a catch-22 that comes with understanding your purpose, capital-P or otherwise. Knowing what you wake up for in the morning and aligning your work to it creates unparalleled energy that we can easily conflate with rejuvenation. The flawed logic can turn into long hours and skipped routines, but there is a difference between mania and alignment. True rejuvenation comes from living in step with our higher values—not when we lose ourselves in service of a vision.

Similarly, the notion of purpose is sometimes dangled in front of us as incentive, when the people or organizations behind those incentives haven't yet created the culture necessary to support our purpose without pushing us closer toward the ledge of burnout.

Gib Bulloch, creator of the Accenture Development Program (ADP), found that people would willingly take a substantial pay cut to do social impact work. ADP ended up becoming a profitable line of business by offering people the chance to walk away from high-paying salaries in exchange for low-value, high-"purpose" work. The salary is rarely what drives us as Catalysts, and we will often leap at the chance to do paid work that aligns with our purpose. We can leap so hard when we get the chance to live in alignment with our purpose that it can lead to very real burnout.

Gib wrote his book, *The Intrapreneur: Confessions of a Corporate Insurgent*, to break the seal around the "taboo" topic of mental health, work, and change agents. He describes how working towards his purpose ultimately led to a burnout so hard, he was hospitalized for mental health issues.

It's not that companies or leaders are intentionally trying to take advantage of letting people do purpose driven work (though that we can't say it's never happened, either). The reality is, unfortunately, that purpose-driven work is often not as handsomely rewarded as other kinds of work. Use your awareness and intuition to pay attention. Don't let your joy of bringing your purpose into work actually accelerate your decline into burnout. And just because the system has historically not paid top dollar for impact work doesn't mean you shouldn't ask for it. You're creating real change, and that change has value.

There is a way to live our purpose at work, still get paid *well*, and be externally successful, *and* not burn out from it. This begins with a more nuanced understanding of our purpose, and equal commitment to supporting our full selves, including a commitment to rejuvenation.

CAPITAL-P PURPOSE

Unfortunately, we have no formula for you on this topic. We don't have a set of steps that will part the heavens and shine a golden light on the thing you're put on this planet to achieve. In fact, not everyone believes we even have a capital-p *Purpose*. It borders on the spiritual, which shows up so very differently for everyone that any given Catalyst might just as likely be drained and beaten down by the need for Purpose as another is energized by it.

If you're one of those people who's been lucky enough to find their calling, congratulations. Few people, in the scheme of things, will be lucky enough to stumble upon this level of purpose in their lifetimes. A rejuvenation practice for you will be more than just working well—having a routine protects your ability to live out your Purpose.

If you don't yet know what your life is meant for, or if you're climbing a mountain range of varied purposes instead of one giant peak—again, congratulations. Your journey will come with incredible peaks and difficult valleys, but you're not alone in them. Rejuvenation for you will remind you that, no matter how many times you rappel down the side of another shifted objective, the climb doesn't define you. You are safe and free to explore, as long as you give yourself the mental, physical, and emotional space to do so.

EVERYDAY PURPOSE

Even if capital-p Purpose has not emerged for you, being clear on your purpose in what you are pursuing now can help you clarify what to say yes to and what to say no to, as well as help people with similar goals magnetize toward you.

A simple but significant question to ask yourself, especially in the context of work, is why you're there.

Why are you in that role, in that moment, showing up to do that work?

This kind of purpose may be easier to define than an overarching Purpose, though it still may not feel easy. Even if your answer is just *for now*, spend time on that question and get clear on your answer before you pose it to others.

When you can identify an overarching Purpose or an everyday purpose *for now*, sharing that with your network and your team opens the door for similar insights in the people around you. Claim your purpose as statement in your bio or on your LinkedIn profile. Incorporate it into your work and talk about how it shapes your time outside of work. That level of authenticity enables others to tap into their sense of purpose and become more comfortable prioritizing it. A group of people prioritizing the things that energize them will thrive in a way that product-oriented teams cannot.[21]

Shannon modeled this with a previous team as she created something new in the organization. First, people shared their personal purposes, then the group created a shared purpose as a team. The entire organization walked through this purpose-seeking exercise. When the managers knew what was driving their employees, it wasn't to hold it over their heads—it became a way to shape a culture that supported each contributor's purpose.

Every time someone new joined the team, Shannon would share her purpose and then she would ask the new team member to share theirs. Each varying Purpose and purposes would go into a bio and up on the wall so that everyone could see who they were working with and what brought them together. The team leaned in *hard*, to collaboratively create

---

21   The work of researcher Linda Hill demonstrates that teams tasked with innovation thrive when they have a shared sense of purpose, values, and rules of engagement. Linda A. Hill, Greg Brandeau, Emily Truelove, and Kent Lineback, "Collective Genius," *Harvard Business Review*, June 2014, https://hbr.org/2014/06/collective-genius.

a purpose built culture, and supporting each other in ways they might not have, had they not understood what made their colleagues light up.

PROTECT THE ROUTINE

We tend to live under the illusion that if we put in one more hour, it will help push the change forward. However, the truth is, our brain can support us in being better changemakers if we make the hard decision to *stop* working. When we create space in our day for things that aren't work and commit to holding that space and protecting the routine, we're able to be more creative and capable.

A 2013 literature review in the journal *Scientific American* illustrates how mental breaks actually increase productivity. One study highlighted had two groups of people analyze information about four different cars—one that was given four minutes before solving simple, unrelated puzzles, while the other was given eight full minutes to deliberate on *just* the task at hand. The group who spent more time on the unrelated activity came up with better choices—to a statistically relevant degree.[22] Why? Because our brain is our ally in the ability to solve problems. It's working with and for us even when we haven't set it to the task of the problem at hand. Such a vital working partner deserves care and inclusion in that process, which looks like brain breaks and rejuvenation routines.

For as uncomfortable as it is to stop working and take a break— whether that's another challenge, a game on your phone, an

---

22 Ferris Jabr, "Why Your Brain Needs More Downtime," *Scientific American*, October 15, 2013, https://www. scientificamerican.com/article/mental-downtime.

actual puzzle, or just a quick walk outside—we don't have to take it upon ourselves to push through to an answer before making space to breathe. Instead we can let our brains work on it behind the scenes while we consciously rest and recover. We already know this is possible from all the times an answer came to us in the shower, in conversation with a friend, or watching a movie.

Spaciousness makes our vision clearer, our actions more decisive, and our ability to listen to feedback and iterate accordingly that much more powerful.

There is no set of activities that universally gives a Catalyst reprieve. We're all very different, spanning all industries, roles, interests, and levels of introversion or extroversion. Before we talk about a routine itself, understand that we mean a set of energy-giving activities that you commit to regularly. Knowing what kind of energy, or rejuvenation, an activity creates helps us apply it to our stressors with precision.

Athletes build in cycles of stress and recovery, while Catalysts don't typically think about their drive toward change with the same intentionality. An athlete in training will systematically stress one area, then allow recovery. If an athlete were to stress one muscle over and over again, it would push their body to its literal breaking point. Yet we push our mental and emotional capacities far beyond their limits and then celebrate it as though it's necessary. There is wisdom in moving in and out of stress rather than forging on regardless of warning signs.

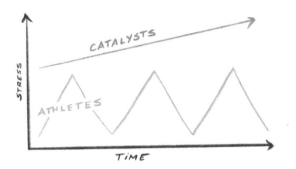

Generally speaking, rejuvenating activities might fall in one of five categories, intended to correspond to the kind of stressor we've been dealing with:

- Destressing and anxiety reduction
- Energy replenishment
- Gaining clarity and connecting dots
- Taking a brain break
- Connecting your head, body, and spirit

DE-STRESS/ REDUCE ANXIETY   ENERGY REBOOT   GAIN CLARITY/ CONNECT DOTS   TAKE A BRAIN BREAK   CONNECT HEAD, BODY & SPIRIT

Within each of those groupings, the activities themselves could be wildly different. A hard run might reduce stress for one person while another would never consider it. While there is a universal benefit to being out in nature, how you engage with nature is up to you.

If you've been under intense stress in a single day, turning to a stress-relieving activity will counter that work. If your energy is buzzing through the mania of early change, something to balance it out and bring you back into your body and self might be useful. Turning from being hunched over a computer working on reports to being slumped over a phone playing a game won't give you the same kind of energy as an activity that shifts your body and mind completely and gives the stressed-out parts a break.

Once you've identified a set of activities that give energy in the right ways, begin to think about how key activities will fit into a routine. Keep in mind how easy it is to let go of yoga class or the gym, nights out with friends, calling mom, actual weekends, proper sleep—especially when it feels like the energy has balanced out and "it's fine" or "it's just this once." But it's incredibly difficult to start new habits and routines, and letting it go might mean never getting it back.

Put rejuvenation on your calendar and treat those blocks of time with as much priority as any meeting or work obligation. Donna is masterful about holding her yoga practice even when she's out of town—when we treat our calendared rejuvenation time seriously, very little can actually stop us from using that time for ourselves. That doesn't mean we won't intentionally move the time now and then, or burn out even when we're holding that space. It's simply another way to prioritize activities and practices that drive change without us so readily losing ourselves.

Remember, the work that you're doing to sustain your energy is just as valid as anything else, if not more so. Protect it, never minimize it, and see how your capacity to work well changes.

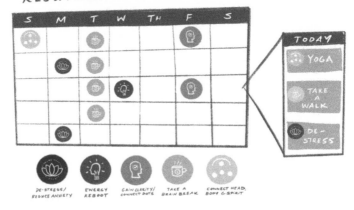

DRAFT A LIST OF ENERGY-REGULATING ACTIVITIES

If you've been keeping track of moments in your day that create or deplete energy, you're a step ahead on this tool. The next step is to turn your catalytic lens inward to solve the problem of energy regulation: What is your vision for an ideal routine, and how quickly can you start testing and iterating through those activities until it's established?

It might help to make a list to draw from when you aren't sure what to try next. A starting point, by no means inclusive or applicable to every Catalyst, might look like this:

> Being in nature, exercise, eating good foods, sleeping well, time with friends or family, short brain breaks, meditation, hot bath or shower, date night, volunteering, knitting, painting, sculpting, cooking, vacation, listening to or making music, reading, spa days, play pick-up sports...

How (or if) you use the items on this list doesn't matter as much as how *intentionally* you use them. Think of it as a change you want to manifest rather than an obligation you have to undergo. Imagine how good it will feel! Shifting the lens in this way allows us to use the tools and skills we've worked so hard to develop—for *us*. Empathy turns into self-compassion, orchestration turns to deep listening to our instincts, and knowing that we're in an iteration stage allows us to play with possibility.

From the onset, you might decide a gym class has to happen every Tuesday morning at ten. But after a week or two of missing it, you realize it's too close to when you drop your daughter off for school, so you're always running late and feeling too rushed to stop and enjoy the workout. So you listen to the cues that say it's not going to work, refuse to beat yourself up about it, and try for another time or activity that will be more feasible.

Again, put them on your calendar. Block them out and commit to them the way you would a work engagement or date with a friend. Maybe even try adding an accountability partner to your calendar invites—give them permission to hold you to that time by asking them to gently remind or encourage you to make that gym class or keep your date with your friends.

Your ideal routine doesn't have to snap into place all at once. It's ok to do a piece at a time. And it's ok to have small moments of rejuvenation throughout your day, rather than big chunks that are static. The energy gained from each piece will carry you into discovering the next piece.

MAKE THE COMMITMENT NON-NEGOTIABLE

We talk about routine more than individual self-care pieces because we so easily lose sight of what gives us energy outside of the work. The mania of a new project isn't negative or unproductive, but it's only a moment in time along the journey of a project. A routine sustains energy regardless of the stage we're in.

Sometimes, your routine will look like a commitment to regularly scheduled activities that you know are important to maintain. Meals, workouts, sleep, and time with family and friends can all fall into this category. Another angle might simply be scheduling time for breaks, during which you're free to counter stress with care. If you're in meetings all day with a lot of tension and conflict, what might balance that stress? If you're feeling tight and wound up, what helps you feel loose and relaxed? That might mean an impromptu workout or some time painting the sunset. The routine is an enabling constraint—it's a boundary, but one that should give you freedom to do what's necessary to recover energy.

Sacrificing the core elements of your routine will come back to haunt the bigger work you're trying to manifest. It will accelerate your path to burnout. It will make you show up in less than desirable ways with the people you want to bring along your journey. The story of sacrifice and constant crisis is one that we tell ourselves is necessary, productive, and good. It's not.

Part of our core company values at Catalyst Constellations is to have fun. You don't have to be miserable in order to serve your vision.

That extra hour of sleep or the evening run or the time on the phone with a friend isn't going to take from work you could be doing—it's going to make you more resilient for what's coming the next day. And even if that doesn't feel true, you only get one wild, precious life. It's ok to just enjoy it now and then.

Prioritize your routine above all else, so you can show up in a way that feels good and will make you more successful. Working well is not just about a successful outcome but about living well as you do it. Rejuvenation is how we make that happen.

LEADING CHANGE: GROUP REJUVENATION

Giving our teams permission to show up as their whole, best selves begins with us doing the same. Not only is there a place for rejuvenation practices in the workplace, but we argue they are necessary if we want our teams to work well. It might start with reminding people to use their vacation days, team offsites and walking meetings outdoors, and it can expand into deeper, more holistic practices as you become comfortable with them.

It's important to name what you're doing and why it's important. Tell them out loud that you want them to have balance as a person, and that you're creating space for rejuvenation to make that possible.

When Tracey works with teams, she often opens with a DiSC assessment exercise first thing. She immediately gets people up out of their seats moving to different corners based on answers to fun questions: Mountains or ocean? Bubbly water or still? Cats or dogs? It gets the room moving physically, laughing, and interacting with each other before moving into questions about how they work and what they care about. As the exercise builds, each person gets closer to who they are as well as the people they can relate to and others they needed to know more about. It creates vulnerability, movement, and intention—and most importantly, it feels right coming from Tracey's background in research.

Shannon opens in completely different ways. No matter who she's working with, all of her team meetings start with an arrival moment not unlike a brief meditation. She's done this for white-collar Texans and blue-collar industrial workers. Each of them are asked to become still, to breathe, to leave behind the noise that had followed them into the room, and to set an intention for how they wanted to show up. Stepping into it with confidence and ownership helps everyone else relax and trust the process that you're laying out for them. They're following your leadership, and before anyone knows it you have a room full of people from diverse backgrounds practicing meditation.[23]

Together, the offerings we develop center around various breaks for rest, presence, and (re)connecting us to our bodies after the deep cerebral processing we've asked Catalysts to do. As a Catalyst leader, it's important to remember that bold visions and change require time and energy reserves for rejuvenation. It's what holds us at the intersection of creativity and strategy, making room for vision and developing trust for orchestration—no matter how uncomfortable it seems at first.

---

23   We fully realize this still sounds intimidating. Tracey wasn't sure about it until she saw Shannon do it live and in person. While we'd love to have you on our team and in our meetings, the next best thing will be the video of one of these openers in our online classes.

The same rejuvenation practices that give *you* space to work will likely benefit your non-catalytic coworkers as well. Modeling mindfulness and rejuvenation practices within the workplace creates an environment that supports catalytic work. What ultimately makes space for *you* is also what creates space for change.

Get outside once a week to walk in nature instead of sitting in the office for the meeting. Hold meditation practices before you begin. Be open about your purpose and ask others about theirs. Be conscious of meeting spaces and how light and open they are. Choose offsites with views and open light rather than the bottom floor of a Hilton. Prepare to advocate for these choices to leadership who might not yet understand.

Rejuvenating practices create spaciousness for everyone, and that ultimately leads to a sense of safety that few of us have experienced in the workplace. We've seen high-powered people break down crying as they talk about their traumas. We've held space as male executives shared about the love and connection that motivates them, with tears rolling down their cheeks. We've walked into rooms filled with contention, led a meditative exercise, and watched as creativity and openness came back into the space.

The most remarkable manifestation of this level of space is when your resistors begin to break down as well. Not necessarily so much that all resistance is gone, but enough that you begin to see each other as collaborators, individuals, and whole human beings once again.

There is a false dichotomy of work life and personal life that is damaging for everyone. It's not as simple as leaving work, going home to rejuvenate, and then coming back. When we're depleted at work, we're depleted at home. Our work suffers, yes, but so does everything else in life. We cannot have a work self and a personal self, so we cannot expect that one won't affect the other. This became painfully evident in 2020, as the lines between work and home were completely erased. We lost all of the resources and structures that made it easier to compartmentalize work, self, home, and school, and were left to grapple with life as it happened, all at once. And on top of it all, we lost access to gyms, parks, and nights out that would otherwise create rejuvenation.

If there's one thing to take from this strange time in history—and there is certainly more than that—it would be that intense integration of all parts of ourselves. Hopefully, this time will help us see each other as whole people, with messy, imperfect lives, allowing us to adopt more energy sustaining practices during work hours and beyond.

This is so much more than self-care. This is protecting your superpowers. It's recognizing the kryptonite instead of deciding you've lost your strengths. It's making sure you don't get taken down by a stray hit while you're busy knocking everyone else's bullets from the air. It's working well, from every possible angle.

If you can't be motivated toward rejuvenation for your own sake just yet, do it for the people around you and the change that's just around the corner. And in any way that you can, reach out to other Catalysts and supporters. We'll hold that space for you until you're ready for more.

REJUVENATION TOOLBOX

- ☐ **Monitor your Energy Tank.** Pay attention to activities that fill your energy tank and begin to lessen or eliminate activities that drain it.

- ☐ **Establish psychological safety**. Create an environment that is safe for iteration and risk-taking through practices around listening, slowing down, allowing for diverse opinions along with modeling and celebrating appropriate failures. Conversely, assess whether the environment you're in is psychologically safe enough to stay.

- ☐ **Practice Mindful Self-Compassion**. Offer forgiveness and understanding to yourself first, so that you can then better offer it to others, through MSC-based practices of self-compassion, awareness, empathy, and intentional pauses.

- ☐ **Reconnect to purpose**. Spend time thinking about your purpose—if not capital-P, at least in the moment—and revisit it whenever you feel like you're spinning your wheels.

- ☐ **Protect the routine**. Turn your Catalyst powers inward to iterate a routine that maximizes energy-giving time and allows you to balance stress with relief. Prioritize that routine above all else, even when the manic stage of change feels like it's giving back.

PART III

THE CATALYST REALIZED

CHAPTER 8

THE POWER OF THE CONSTELLATION

 "At some point, you'll realize that it's your time to do something, and because of the constellation around you, *only* you can do it. If you back down, there won't be another opportunity. The time is now."

Saidah was the VP, Mobile Strategy & Innovation at the New York headquarters for Thomson Reuters, with a volunteer role as Global Co-Chair of the Black Employee Network in 2015. Just two years after Trayvon Martin's killer was acquitted and the Black Lives Matter movement came to the forefront, one year after Eric Garner's "I can't breathe" seared our collective consciousness and four years before George Floyd would echo him. That summer brought Rachel Dolezal pretending to be Black within a senior role in the NAACP and Dylan Roof's mass murder inside of a historically Black church. All hell had broken loose.

While certain things aren't spoken of in an office setting—race, money, religion—Saidah and the other leaders in her network knew they couldn't afford silence in their position within the Black Employee Network. She describes the sense of tumultuousness within the Black community in the midst of systemic violence: "So many Black men and boys were being shot down and strangled in the streets, and it was happening with greater frequency, made painfully and visually available on social media." When an employee came to her in utter pain and frustration, asking if they could just have a conversation, she knew it was time.

Saidah had a good sense for their C-Level executive positions on race relations and commitment to diversity which was always forward thinking and supportive, but the resistance showed up in surprising ways when she stepped into action. "I don't think they had any idea what we were really going to do," she said. And how could they? The network decided to host an open conversation around race, held on the thirtieth floor of the Thomson Reuters offices in Times Square—the site of their most prestigious events. "The resistance we felt from the very beginning, from some unexpected places, was shocking. And we decided to do it anyway."

Because Saidah had spent years building relationships within the company, she knew who to tap into and rely on for gut checks as they spent a year planning the event. Without that support, the air-cover from relationships in the C-Suite, and the persistence needed to push past resistance, the event might have been stopped. They had to move forward even with high profile people still in resistance, which underscored even further the need for connection. "I was more glad than ever to be a co-chair, because that meant I had a partner in it. We talked constantly for months, always checking in with each other and circling up on our conversations." They needed each other's support as they experienced the grief and emotions that their colleagues were feeling, while going up against executives who had "massive blind spots" in this area.

Few were doing anything like this at the time, and certainly not in such a high-profile way.

The CEO introduced the event. Head of People and the General Counsel were in attendance. The speaker was an academic from Harvard, who handled the difficult topic brilliantly. He used humor and facts in a way that felt congenial without diluting the power of the message. Afterward, some of the people who were staunchly against the event changed their tune. It was a clear success that didn't stop once the lights went out. Many conversations followed that first event. "But the journey to the first one was littered with blood, sweat, and tears, quite literally," Saidah recalls.

It took significant social and political capital for Saidah to pull those strings and make that event happen, and she points to a larger sense of purpose that made it possible. With the violence ongoing, a place for support is vital. "These tragedies take place and get into our homes and communities on a Monday, absolutely devastating us, and we have to show up on Tuesday as if nothing happened at all." Saidah's unique position and connections gave her a platform to create new openness and support where there had once been avoidance. People of color and Black Americans in particular show up to work in an environment that's dismissive or openly hostile about their trauma, and she and the Black Employee Network opened up space to hold some of that burden.

"Sadly," she notes, "police brutality against young men of color didn't end because we held some event on the thirtieth floor in Times Square." But that's, essentially, the point. Knowing that these tragedies aren't just going to go away, Saidah and her network set out to create space in the workplace for employees to respond when it happens. We cannot predict how or when trauma will hit, and when it does, everyone should have access to someone who understands what they're going through. Saidah used her connections to open that door and create that space for emotional safety that would allow employees of color to thrive in the face of global shared trauma, and it will forever be her legacy within that organization.

Between her supporters within the organization and personal support outside of it, Saidah credits her resilience to connection. The Black Employee Network found leverage with other groups working toward equality, like women's leadership and LGBT groups, to identify areas to work together on shared priorities. But on a more personal level, Saidah relied on the support she and her co-sponsor Jackie provided each other. The network was focused on creating a larger support structure, but Saidah and Jackie needed each other if they were going to see the vision through.

"Some of it was very messy," Jackie confided. Emotions run high in a space like this, and Jackie and Saidah would keep each other grounded or buoyant, depending on the circumstance. "That connection, when you're really able to spot each other like that, was the secret sauce to our success."

Saidah encourages Catalysts to find their own support networks, particularly in the midst of significant change.

"Surround yourself with people who know you and support you and support what you're working on." Find support in your organization and outside of it. Find support at home. Find supporters of your catalytic work and supporters of your Catalyst self.

The work is not easy, but it's ours. Connection supercharges our superpowers to maximize impact and sustain us through it. Get seen and connected, hold each other up as Catalysts, and find or create support within your organization—the time is now.

THE CATALYST CONNECTED

We've brought forward tools to help you better build influence and utilize your Network Map as you catalyze new change, but Saidah's story points to something deeper than orchestration. The ultimate goal is not to find people who can do things for you but to connect deeply with others around shared needs and solutions.

Saidah's journey shows us just how vital connection is on a person-to-person basis as well as to facilitate change—from the way she and her co-chair supported each other during difficult moments, to the structures they created to help their colleagues recover from trauma—and the tools in Part II will help you maximize that change. But in the remainder of this chapter, we're going to focus on connection as a form of rejuvenation.

The model of Maslow's Hierarchy depicted our basic human needs as a stack of hierarchical priorities. If your needs were met, in an ascending order, eventually you could reach self-actualization. Remove things like belonging or safety, and the whole structure would topple.

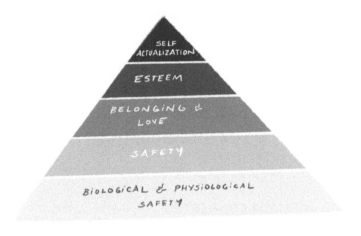

Maslow was on to something—however, our various needs as humans all more or less orbit around the primary need for human connection. That means, when we move too fast for others to follow, break shit without mindful awareness of how that affects our surroundings, and push ourselves into isolated burnout over and over again, the repeated loss of connection strips away our ability to be effective anywhere else.

Maslow's hierarchy feels more accurate to our context if it's re-imagined to acknowledge the fundamental role that connection plays in our well-being. No matter how aware we become of our formula, strengths, and weaknesses, we have to plug into connection in order to power the entire system.

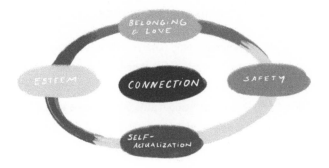

If you haven't experienced community in the way we have described, you might not yet know how deeply you need it. The relief that comes from a group of people who understand you—or just having a really good conversation with a kindred spirit—is unmatched by any other practice.

Connection is the thing that we need more than any other structural supports for creativity and change. It's the sun that we orbit around. And for Catalysts, being surrounded by other Catalysts is nothing short of miraculous.

Almost every week as new Catalysts join our community, someone breaks down in tears. The depth of relief and release from being seen and understood in a way they may never have experienced before is—in their words, not ours—"life changing." People describe it as "coming home."

In a world where we have been isolated, called names, often bullied, and experienced trauma because of our inherent Catalyst qualities, stepping into a space where people like you get you is incredibly healing. You can finally let your true Catalyst flag fly high and proud. And the community leans in hard to provide support. To support *you*.

PAUSE WITH TRACEY

During the initial research, some Catalysts shared stories of catalytic tendencies dating back to childhood. When that happens, it isn't with the same energy that some Catalysts might talk about their lemonade stand or an athlete might talk about little league. Instead of inspiration and belonging, that subset of Catalysts relayed a profound sense of loneliness.

They didn't want to play the same games that other kids played. They didn't share the same interests. Sometimes, their families of origin disparaged them for being different or too ambitious or "too much." A great deal of pain comes forward with this lone wolf persona.

I noted this recurring theme as I worked with Catalysts but didn't acknowledge it in myself or act on it—until Shannon came along as I was digging into the research on Catalysts. When she mentioned the idea of a retreat in our conversation, it almost threw me off my interview game. The ongoing theme of loneliness that I heard in my clients and experienced as an individual consultant and coach all came crashing down at once because Shannon's suggestion was such a clear solution that I had not even considered. When she invited me to join her, it felt like our puzzle pieces had come together. I needed her as a natural connector to help me find my people—not just for me but for all of us.

Not every Catalyst is a natural connector, and not every Catalyst grew up feeling lonely and unseen. But when we come together, online or in person or now and then over a quick email, we create something for each other that the rest of the world doesn't quite understand. For me, having a community is having a place to put my big energy and ideas and power, where people will encourage me to think bigger rather than running away scared because of it. I feel at equilibrium in a group of

Catalysts in a way I had no inkling was possible. It will mean something different for you—and you'll have something beautiful and big and wild of your own to give back. And all of us together, standing in our light, become a beacon for other lone wolves to make their way home.

THE POWER OF BEING SEEN

Since the beginning of time, humanity has looked to the stars for some clue to our existence. They aren't part of life on earth. We can't touch or even see them as they truly are, but we feel close to them anyway. Instead of shrinking away from the existential reality of our smallness, we stared into the unknown and found stories. We have connected the blinking dots in the sky and found reflections of ourselves.

Sometimes, it's hard to admit that we belong as a Catalyst. Do we really fit in with big doers accomplishing great things in the world? After so long not fitting in anywhere, the premise that we're not alone sounds too good to be true.

But you're still with us at this point for a reason. Something in you says you belong. The dots are connecting. The story is taking shape. You've seen your patterns of the past. Now it's time to look to the future. And the truth that you're powerful instead of broken is too good *not* to be true.

When we bring Catalysts together, from retreats to courses to meetings to gatherings, we start with introductions and stated intentions. What are we hoping to create or untangle from our time together? What big problems are we working through? What can we keep each other accountable to as we move in and out of work and rejuvenation?

At first, saying your brand-new baby idea out loud can be scary, and we can be unclear because of it. We're more used to being shot down than we are to coming to clarity. But in the space of acceptance that Catalysts create for each other, you soon see that your idea is honored, and people are excited, curious, and hungry to know more. As you give that idea space to breathe, and as other Catalysts feed and nourish it, those small ideas quickly grow and take shape and come into focus as something that might be achievable.

Connection makes being a Catalyst feel possible, real, and amazing. When someone *else* sees you and those strengths you hold, it's the most powerful gift they can give. We are your fellow creators, and we're all in this together.

CONNECTING WITH OTHER CATALYSTS

There are lots of places you can find other Catalysts. Now that you can articulate it, you've probably already run through your mental Network Map and identified a few. You might be a Catalyst who's introverted or extroverted, talkative or quiet, an executive or at an early stage in your career.

The label of Catalyst isn't meant to prescribe behavior or filter out personality types. There is no baseline minimum threshold of energy or productivity that lets you in the door. When you find people who drop into deep ideas quickly, aren't put off by your thought pacing, and don't shrink away from the work you want to do—you know. It's like a weight taken off of your shoulders.

If connection is what we orbit, there is a sense of gravity around Catalysts that pulls us to each other along the way.

We're going to find other Catalysts—it's just a matter of how much potential power we will create in those relationships.

Being able to connect with other people who see and understand us is a gamechanger for our experience and energy. If you don't already have that network, we have one ready for you. We have the training, coaching, mentoring, and small groups necessary for you to thrive. If you sit in an organizational context and would like to systematically find and support Catalysts, we can help you with that, too. Our ambition is to help you identify Catalysts, bring them together, and give them support and help you do some of the heavy lifting of getting executives to understand, support, and value Catalysts. This can be one of the heaviest emotional challenges for Catalysts, and we're here to help.

SHOWING UP WELL FOR OTHER CATALYSTS

Building a supportive network can be seen as a challenge to tackle. It's a new change to make, and that comes with every step of the Catalyst's journey that we've worked through to this point. All of the pitfalls and tools and pausing and slowing down will be just as important when working with other Catalysts as they are in your day to day.

Even when a network is in place, intentionality will be the key to keeping it alive. Catalysts aren't going to thrive on a weekly coffee meeting without any kind of purpose. Make decisions together about what the group is intended to accomplish and whether it is still meeting that objective. If it begins to lose its effectiveness, make the decision to pause or disband just as intentional as well. Turn your catalytic lens inward as often as possible to optimize your support of each other and the work you're trying to do.

Practice the tools here just as you would in any other manifested change. They are meant to help you work well *together* just as much as they help you work well in unsupported environments. Slipping into old habits of unconscious, unintentional action runs the risk of tarnishing the name of Catalyst. We have to walk the talk first before jumping in and creating too much disruption.

Active listening exercises are especially important, because it's just as critical to be heard and to learn how to truly listen to others as it is to be seen. When you feel like you always have the answer, it's hard to hear what the other person is actually saying. When you feel like you're never heard, it's hard to believe the other person is actually listening to you.

Working with other Catalysts isn't the same as working with anyone else. Mindfulness in every interaction will help you supercharge that connection and more powerfully move the world forward.

And you only have to connect with a group of Catalysts once to know just how sincerely we use the word "power" here.

Alone, we can create remarkable change in the world. But when you step into a space where the others in the room see you in all of your strengths, can relate to all of your downfalls, and will stand by you as you make messes and break shit, it's like a breath of fresh air. When we come together for accountability to be more intentional and encouragement to think bigger, it's like rocket fuel in our energy tanks.

And together, we're unstoppable.

BETTER TOGETHER: CREATING CONNECTION

- ☐ Connect with Catalysts and supporters at work to help birth and co-create ideas.
- ☐ Connect with people at work to help activate change.
- ☐ Connect with your boss to establish safety and create accountability to your formula.
- ☐ Connect with partners, family, and friends outside of work to refill your energy tank.
- ☐ Connect with Catalysts outside of work who aren't locked into the same system and can help you see and imagine outside the cultural context.
- ☐ In the back of the book and on our website, we have some conversation starters that can help you initiate these conversations to create connection, including articulating your strengths and verbalizing your needs. We are also constantly developing new ways for Catalysts to connect via www.CatalystConstellations.com.

CHAPTER 9

OWN YOUR SUPERPOWERS

 How can a government office be made to feel welcoming? How can its people feel like they belong, like they are respected, and not just another number? This wasn't Virginia's original mandate in the Department of Labor. Her role as a Regional Administrator under the Obama Administration was to make sure the billions of dollars that the federal government allocated to the states along the West Coast were distributed properly. Because of the department, the programs included unemployment insurance, public workforce systems, programs for migrant farm workers, kids coming out of foster care, and people who have been in the criminal justice system. And she was executing that role at the height of the Great Recession.

Recalling an old *Nightline* special on IDEO's use of design thinking to redesign a shopping cart, of all things, Virginia made catalytic connections that no one had made before. With a vision to bring human-centered design to government work, Virginia negotiated a two-week contract with IDEO, bringing together leaders from the state of California and

Washington, kindred spirits whom she trusted to help create something new, and the team at IDEO. They started with a two-day workshop digging into who their "customers" were and how they could be best served in such a challenging time.

The biggest insight that came out of that workshop was just how much emotion was at play for their customers, and how little emotion government agencies paid attention to. Government employees were focused on compliance with rules, not with how people were feeling. But with people coming in about to lose their car or house or apartment if they couldn't access assistance, human-centric connection was vital. The last thing they wanted was a workshop on networking and resume-writing. Every person seeking assistance had a different story.

"The person who sent out hundreds of resumes into the black hole of the internet is different from the person whose occupation has literally gone away. They are all different people with different emotions. But our agencies were treating them all the same."

The solutions they mocked up were innovative enough that IDEO wanted to take them back to DC for a bigger contract—but Virginia knew they weren't ready. She had already faced some resistance around the way she wanted to stretch outside of her mandate. It had already taken some bold moves, speaking outside of her rank to the Secretary of Labor when given the chance and telling the truth whenever asked. But to take it to DC, she needed more evidence, more anecdotes, more stories that could make their case. By what she considers to be a miracle, Congress passed the Workforce Innovation and Opportunity Act with bipartisan agreement. It was the perfect cover for her to bring up her case studies and hypotheses, in the name of innovation. And she wasn't about to waste that opportunity.

She connected with people in the White House and shared her vision to use design thinking to implement the new law. Now way outside of her mandate and pay grade, she helped issue challenges to agencies around the country. "Let's put them through training, then we can invite the ones who do well with it to the White House for a celebration."

They launched with White House officials on board and visibly lending credibility to the effort. People in DC started to pay attention. Her boss allocated funding to help her teams through the process. On launch day, when Virginia expected to have a dozen or fewer teams sign up after the initial webinar, eighty teams from around the country were present, and eleven came to the celebration. A second time around, 120 teams signed up.

California went on to invest a half million dollars in training for local organizations who wanted to implement the practices. Washington put nine hundred people through a LUMA Institute innovation class.

From the seeds of an idea, to bold moves, to quick action when the opportunity presented itself, Virginia had developed a new way for government offices to view themselves and their work—and it exploded. After that, Virginia opened up a conference program with her keynote on design thinking for a crowd of around eight hundred people. During the Q&A portion, Virginia recalls a woman in the back voicing the concerns she had in the beginning—what happens when oversight agencies block us up?

Virginia stepped out from behind the podium, stood in front of the room, and blew all of their minds:

"My name is Virginia Hamilton. I'm the regional administrator for the US Department of Labor, and I'm hereby giving you permission to experiment to make the services to your customers better."

The crowd rose to their feet in a standing ovation.

The power of permission—the safety, acceptance, and support to do what needs to be done—cannot be understated. People who come out of her training tell her how she saved their careers and changed their lives. How they were ready to quit, but being able to connect with their customers again changed their perspective and gave them new energy. Virginia and her team weren't just adding processes. They saw the future of work and brought it into the present, within their context.

Virginia's work as a Catalyst is the epitome of VUCA Prime. While the recession and housing crisis introduced mass amounts of volatility, uncertainty, complexity, and ambiguity, Virginia looked beyond the metrics and to the heart of the issue. Her vision for change introduced vulnerability and understanding in place of faceless processes. While hindsight tells her she could have been clearer in articulating the vision, she stepped into action in a way that enabled agility in the people around her.

STANDING IN OUR STRENGTHS

Since we don't all have a Virginia Hamilton paving the way in our industries, sometimes we have to give ourselves the permission to experiment that we so desperately want from our organizations. We know that, like it or not, VUCA is the future of work and Catalysts are ready to adapt. We are on our way there, while our organizations are often lagging behind. Because we are out in front paving the way, it's up to us to own our powers, articulate them, and advocate for them.

It's up to us to stand in our strengths, because not everything that's valuable can be tracked with metrics.

For example, take sports analysts, who are meticulous with their metrics. Watch almost any game for ten minutes and you'll see half a dozen different stats pop up. However, there is no metric for the "glue guy," despite the value that person can bring to a team.

These are the role players who rarely show up in the stats sheet but do a range of small things that make the team better. It's the wide receiver who can block well or the shooting guard who is a great defender but scores less than ten points in a game. Glue guys are the players who see the way the game is working and do what's necessary to get the team a win, even if it doesn't improve their individual stats much at all.

We're the glue, and our metrics are just as nuanced.

Sometimes, they're written off as "soft skills"—a term that's used to sideline people like us, even though they are integral to our collective genius, spaciousness, and ability to move forward.

Sure, we need to generate results. We need the bottom line to move. We need, we need, we need—but how do we get those things?

Through people. Through systems change. Through deep listening and high-level connections.

Through Catalysts.

Organizations have already started to call for VUCA readiness—leaders who can help them move through the volatility, uncertainty, complexity, and ambiguity of our world. Our new reality does not align with our old ways of being, and flexibility is the new pace of the world. Companies know they have to train their people in this direction. So why don't we see a better reception for the individuals who are not only VUCA ready but who thrive in it?

The necessity of catalyticness is all over the literature. The world is changing, and organizations have to think and execute in new ways to be ready. Leaders have to rethink ways of working in light of the gig economy and competition for talent. We have burnout in the World Health's ICD-11 and people learning to set boundaries. We have companies asking millennials to mentor their executives to help them adapt to the new world. Now, we need to connect the problem to the solution.

We believe it's a matter of consciousness.

If our own processes have been unconscious for so long, it's not surprising that they're invisible to others as well.

We need to see ourselves and the other Catalysts we work with for who and what we are and just how powerfully we can move the workplace away from rigidity and into an uncertain but promising future. And then we need to support each other in our work.

When we show up as our whole selves, in organizations that we're aligned to, using the tools that bring our catalyticness to consciousness, there's no limit to what's possible. We can bring our organizations into this new future. We can facilitate the rejuvenation practices that lessen burnout cycles. We can step back to see the efficiency of the system as a whole, from contractors to the C-Suite. We can bring a deeper level of person-to-person empathy into the organization and the direction we're moving.

And the beautiful caveat is that simply showing up as our whole selves is enough, separate from any scale of impact. If all you can do right now is turn your catalytic powers inward to take care of yourself, that's powerful, too. You don't have to be ready to step into every new idea just because you can, and you certainly don't have to carry that burden alone.

Of course, what we all want—what we really need—is for someone to look at us the way we look at the world. We see deeply, and we want to *be seen* deeply.

We revel in feedback about how the process can be optimized or the change could be improved, because that means someone is in it with us, looking for the same things we are—instead of on the outside looking in with criticism.

But until organizations name, value, and support Catalysts, we have an obligation to stand in our strengths. Our focus on the interconnectivity of people and ideas is ahead of the curve in an increasingly integrated world. We provide something valuable to our organizations both in a direct line to the bottom dollar *and* outside of it. And advocating for ourselves is how we advocate for a better future.

SEE YOUR STRENGTHS

Chelsey went up against Google on a culture issue. Shakeya brought her organization's ethics into a global spotlight. Michael is working on a space station, John created a new market segment, Donna taught an old company new techniques, Saidah created space for a community on fire, and Virginia changed the country. And these stories are only a few, together representing billions of dollars in revenue and hundreds of thousands of people combining to make their companies, regions, and world better.

Long before results can be measured, the "magic" of a Catalyst involves work that people rarely see, much less understand, especially if we hand it off for someone else to implement. If we're being honest, we can be blind to our own value as well.

In our interviews with Catalysts, we asked them to describe what makes them feel successful, and they couldn't. As we move fast, we set goals that continue moving and growing, and are always stepping into new scenarios that trigger imposter syndrome. The feeling of success just wasn't strong enough to articulate.

So we reframed it: What do you see as your powers?

That's when we caught them talking about strengths in various ways: connect dots, see the big picture, navigate complexity, practice systems thinking, see vision, analysis, synthesis, high empathy, high EQ, relationship building, and execution. We also saw that Catalysts actually are *aware* of value that we bring to our organizations, but we struggle to articulate it when asked.

Catalysts self-articulated four main values to an organization—that we come to innovative and creative solutions to help companies be competitive long-term, that we tackle challenges across the organization, that we inspire transformation and create movements, and that we work with endurance and speed.

To support that value, Catalysts are able to name strengths that we know we're amazing at (even when we don't say we are). Aggregated, the strengths fall into three main categories: we see into the future, we have strong relationships with people and understand that people are key to making change and we get shit done.

Said another way: Catalysts see what is possible, through and with other people, then make the dream a reality, through and with other people. We are the visionaries *and* the do-ers.

ARTICULATE YOUR VALUE

We take it for granted that everyone can see futures, activate people, and drive results—but that's just not the case. We get shit done in a way that's obvious to us and magic to everyone else. It's not easy to admit, but we're powerful in our own right. If we can get honest with ourselves about who we are and what we bring to the table, then we can learn to translate our superpowers into an organizational context.

A word of caution, however: While this book might have given you language that's helpful for your own understanding, walking into an interview or your boss's office to say, "I'm a Catalyst" likely will not help you articulate your value. You could list the Catalyst's strengths that we've given you here, but we all have our own flavors of catalyticness. If Shannon's flavor is *sushi* while Tracey's is *cheese,* and you could be *chocolate-covered strawberries,* there's a whole lot more left to be described than just "Catalyst," before someone can know what to do with us.

Take some time to think about your personal strengths that may or may not overlap with your catalytic strengths. Yours might be *ideation, analyzing complex information, implementation strategy, building thriving teams,* or *startup management.* There are no wrong answers here, just genuine ones.

There are different ways to build your list. Get a book on strengths.[24] Look at past reviews for the good things people have said. Ask people who you've worked with. Pull from as much data as you can, then aggregate it.

Once you've identified the things you're great at, take a moment to write out two stories from your professional past that show each strength in action. This shifts the dynamic

---

24   One book we suggest here is *StrengthsFinder 2.0* by the Gallup Organization's Tom Rath.

from strengths alone to translating those strengths into something real.

Now, read them out loud to someone—your coach, someone in the Catalyst community, a safe person from your network. Aside from practice speaking your strengths, you'll also get input on how to better translate those values to your organizational context. People don't hire us on the merit of being Catalysts. They hire us because we're willing to use our Catalyst strengths in service of what they want to achieve. They hire us because we solve wicked problems and we get shit done—but there are always going to be different metric settings for Catalysts than our counterparts.

When translating your value to something tangible and contextual, you might start with some reasonable interim metrics before tracking bottom line impact. Shannon did this at Vodafone. They had a certain number of innovation workshops to do for the first few years, and then moved to how many new C-Level relationships they developed for the organization with what kind of NPS, and then finally bottom-line impact. Yet for all of the accomplishments she tracked along the way, it wasn't until the bottom-line came into view that people started to realize just how much her four-person team was doing.

You're going to have to get creative to be seen. Each person in an organization has their own wins outside of just the outwardly articulated goals, as well. A win for a boss may be, "Make me look great in front of senior leadership," and that will be noted whether or not other metrics are achieved. Pay attention to what their rewards and metrics are, and get clear on what yours can and should be as well. Some people enjoy being in the spotlight, while others just want some quiet space for time off. Be specific about what motivates you, so that when you meet the metrics, the win/win can happen—and even then, it may not be enough.

Even though these are not soft skills that we're articulating, they represent an approach to work that society hasn't caught up with yet.

Looking beyond our current VUCA scenarios and seeing how an organization can prepare for the future *is* value.

Actively listening to the needs of the organization and pulling solutions together using empathy and connection *is* value.

Pushing forward with bravery and tenacity in the face of unease and resistance *is* value.

As much as organizations need the tangible, they require the intangible to get there. And, it's important to note, those things cannot be taught in the way that the more visible skills like sales, engineering, or coding can be. Own that. Take the powers that you know you have and turn them toward self-awareness until you can see, own, and articulate your strengths and the value they create.

THE BENEFIT OF COACHING

Being seen is about more than just the feeling. When someone else sits with us in our circumstances without getting mired in them, it gives us a new perspective and added energy for change. Coaches can hold our concerns, issues, and still-muddy problems for us with some distance, like Catalysts working to untangle our mental and emotional space.

If you don't have a coach, asking colleagues specifically to describe your value can bolster confidence in a way that self-perception might miss. One person volunteered, "Someone told me I don't have to be everything, and I have gotten comfortable with that. I'm a starter—I don't have to be a closer."

Having a coach in your corner is an external source of perspective that can help you come to those realizations faster. A coach is a sounding board for the problems that might otherwise turn into an iteration spiral. They can help you catch problems early, avoid unnecessary self-doubt, and help you practice the tools that will help you work well. We'd love to work with you—but the important thing is to make sure you're supported in some way.

IMPOSTER SYNDROME

The flexibility that allows Catalysts to make change almost anywhere—the very thing that makes us valuable within almost any organization—constantly puts us in uncharted territory. We get one thing figured out just to move onto the next, with every doubt and worry that comes with something new.

Our individual work rarely comes with a handbook. We make things up as we go along, putting pieces together that seem to fit but that bump up against the boundaries of what's known, comfortable, and safe. Once resistors and questioners show up like a megaphone for the doubts we've harbored, imposter syndrome is inevitable. Especially when we feel unseen or undervalued for what we do.

By that point, we're often unsupported and alone with our thoughts. And a very different story begins to take shape in our minds. One without super speed or days saved or battles won.

"It seemed so obvious."

"Why can't they see it?"

"Why is it going so slowly?"

"Maybe they're right."

"Does that mean I'm wrong?"

"Maybe my intuition was off."

"Maybe I used up all of my magic."

"Can I defend this?"

"Can I deliver it?"

"Am I really a Catalyst?"

One Catalyst described it as constantly being out on a ledge, inches away from falling off, and reveling in the excitement in spite of the danger. "Meanwhile," she added, "everyone else is down the hill at a party that I started and will never get to attend."

For the Catalyst who is aware of their strengths and using the tools we've worked through here, the doubt is a little easier to address. We can check in with the vision to regain some energy (chapter 4) or follow the breadcrumbs to acknowledge the progress we've made (chapter 5). We can reframe failure and check in with our network for affirmation (chapter 6). We can create distance between who we are and what we do and take care of our whole selves amidst the work (chapter 7).

Here's the catch: if we can become aware of our process and pause frequently to pay attention to the details—we'll *still* face imposter syndrome. We'll still have those doubts, ask those questions, and wonder why anyone trusted us in the first place. Imposter syndrome has a field day with us, no matter how much work we do to combat it. Even though we feel like we've successfully achieved what the organization brought us in to do.

This is a lot of work. Not one of us does it perfectly. It's challenging, and that's what makes it both exhilarating and terrifying. We're always imposters because we're always pushing out toward something new, and we wouldn't have it any other way.

But we have good news. Our research suggests that Catalysts become confident in their value and get comfortable articulating their value over time when we do it with intention. This helps us in our jobs, to get new jobs, to secure funding, in writing books, in building influence... the list goes on. Taking time to get comfortable in your strengths is worth the work.

WHEN OUR POWERS AREN'T ENOUGH

The pauses we advocated for with each of the tools not only give you as the Catalyst space to work well for yourself but to also make the process visible to everyone. The more it can be seen and followed, the better valued it can be.

When a Catalyst is still operating from a place of unconscious competence, those requirements for change are rarely named or acknowledged. We may even see creating big responses as positive because that creates dialogue and action we crave. For some managers or organizations, the disruption that we cause isn't worth the potential change. Especially if we let passion take over when we feel unheard and get desperate, they might view us as toxic to keeping the peace and protecting their hard-won culture. Unless we are well protected, our value may not be worth the expense.

No matter how "right" we are, empathy for others and their experience of us is the most important part of articulating our value—especially when it turns into a removal of support.

It's difficult to detect a loss of support. People won't always tell us that it has happened, and we won't always be able to identify the cause when it does. As strange as it sounds, they might not even know that they've stopped supporting you. While this list is not complete by any means, it can serve as a starting point to help you think carefully about your surroundings and whether you've lost the safety net that will allow you to work your magic without risking your job or invoking further trauma.

- What do my interactions feel like with people in the organization? Have those feelings changed from months past? Has my anxiety increased? Do I feel safe to share or try new things?

- Have I stopped getting traction in an area that had been moving?
- Do people agree with me in meetings and say they will do something, and then go right back to their former behavior?
- Can I still get on the executive calendar when needed?
- Am I spending more time in damage control than on the actual work?
- Am I starting to spin out in a resistance-burnout cycle?
- Have the people who brought me into the organization left?
- If you're spending more time doing damage control, repeating actions, or justifying your value, the chances of being able to move forward in a way that gives you energy are low.

Awareness that our context is constantly changing allows us to balance large visions with a sense of realism—by tailoring every step, every interaction to where we are in the moment.

This work can feel heavy. It's one thing for people to know that they need change management and something else entirely to understand and appreciate the extensive procedural, personal, and interpersonal work that change actually requires. Not only does it require rejuvenation to sustain it, but it's also why we need external support. We need a coach or connection to a network, as well as supporters like a VP of Operations or a Chief of Staff who can help carry the load.

Without an advocate or supporters who will have your back when you begin to iterate or when resistance kicks in, you might not have the psychological safety needed for success. At that point, you will have difficult decisions to make around your own wellbeing, any remaining reasons to stay, and a path forward to protect yourself and your energy as much as possible.

The ability to articulate our process enables us to bring people along with us, even when they value immediate outcomes over extended visions. But without buy-in from leadership, you will be at risk. Bravery won't be enough. Self-advocacy won't be enough. Communication won't be enough. Orchestration won't happen, vision won't be realized, and we won't be likely to make it out without another layer of trauma. Even if they're wrong, and especially if your advocate leaves or is removed.

CATALYST 2.0

The only thing that has really changed from the beginning of this book to now is that we've brought those strengths to consciousness. Without awareness and intention, we can do a lot of good—but we can also do a lot of damage. We don't realize the noise we're creating or the messages we're internalizing. We don't know that we're increasing resistance by making others feel criticized or confused. We don't know how much more is possible because we don't know how we got here in the first place.

Now that you have consciousness around the steps of the process and permission to own the label of Catalyst, your powers are in your hands.

In every phase of change, through every stage of our journey, our connection to the ideas (clarity), empathy for others (connection), and care for ourselves (consistent rejuvenation) serve to drive the change further, hold resistance lower, and push burnout back so that we can continue to work well.

Of course, we're always happy to hear about a new project or change in the works—but what really matters first is whether you'll manifest a new, more powerful version of yourself. Catalyst 2.0, filled with intention and purpose and ability.

Yes, you can use these tools to improve your team. Yes, you can change your organization, even your industry. But what about your routine? Your relationships? The life you want to create?

We give so much energy to the things that will make the world better for people around us that we can forget that we're part of that world, too. We're comfortable declaring audacious goals for everyone but ourselves. When it comes to our vision for a home, a spouse, a friendship, a lifestyle, we turn magical thinking up as high as it will go and just hope it happens.

But you are a Catalyst.

You are a vehicle for magic, and now you know exactly how to drive it.

We're asking you to do some deep, personal work to get to that point. It's healing work. It's empowering work. It's terrifying work.

We're asking you to face the demons that have held you back. Where you've internalized messages about your worth, your weaknesses, and your mistakes until you couldn't separate from them anymore. And then, we're asking you to break them down and replace them with the truth.

Working well is about getting clear, connected, and intentional about who we are and the value we create. That makes self-awareness the most important tool of all. You are the secret weapon. Once you see where you've been playing small, you can't unsee it. This magic won't go back in a box.

If we don't—if we hold onto unconscious competence and magical thinking and frustration that the world just doesn't appreciate us—all of those misperceptions will continue. All of those conflicts will increase. We'll keep moving too fast and losing people. We'll keep breaking shit instead of building the future. And we'll keep burning out, crashing harder every time.

We can't be seen for what we won't own, and we can't own something that we won't acknowledge is there. We can't set expectations when we don't admit how much work we're about to do and the cost to ourselves and people around us. We can't demonstrate empathy when we don't have self-awareness. We can't work well if we don't admit that we do our work *damn* well.

Until we see ourselves, with all of our flaws and strengths—not as imposters but as creators—our powers will be limited. Name them. Own them. Give yourself permission to unleash them.

This is who you were born to be, and that's a good thing. As much as you have compassion for others and want to see their lives improved, you deserve compassion for yourself. To see your life improved. To ground yourself in clarity, immerse in your abilities, and become deeply connected to others who want to see you succeed as much as you want that for others.

To move fast without losing people, break shit with intentionality, and shorten the burnout cycle.

And in case you need to hear it from someone other than yourself:

We are Tracey Lovejoy and Shannon Lucas. We represent Catalysts, and we hereby give you permission to vision the future, bring people together to create it, and iterate until it is made reality.

We see you, Catalyst.

When you see yourself, too, you're going to change the world, in the powerful way that only you can.

RESOURCES

WORKING WITH A
CATALYST 101

*This is a sample set of conversation starters that you might use to help
a boss or co-worker understand more about your process and how to
better support you. Following this page and available as a printable on our
website, there is a template you can use to synthesize your own definitions
and conversation notes.*

Example definitions and strengths: My strengths help you be ready
for the future. I like to tackle meaty problems, see possible solutions,
activate people toward that change and drive hard toward results. I help
organizations stay relevant and competitive in a VUCA world. The organization can get its best value out of me by aligning me to challenges
the organization is trying to solve, that require us to move fast and take
risks without a lot of bureaucracy. I thrive where I can build, transform,
or tear down and turnaround.

Example conversation starters:

→   I'm always looking toward your and the company's success, now
    and in the future. Your sponsorship and ongoing air cover when I
    challenge the status quo is critical to my success, and by extension,
    the success of the organization. Can we regularly partner on the air
    cover that will be helpful at each stage of our project?

→ When working on projects or with teams, I move fast and connect dots quickly. Others should know that they can speak up when I need to slow down to better bring them along. If you see me getting too far in front of the organization, can you please flag that for me and help pull me back?

→ I will make a big investment getting to know and understand you because I believe it will allow us to make aligned decisions faster. I thrive with real-time feedback that is supported with specific examples. Can I ask that you provide me feedback as we go so there are no big surprises?

→ In my experience, new ideas can sometimes be met with resistance and get shut down before consideration. How can we best work together to cultivate psychologically safe private and public places for new ideas to be shared and explored?

→ Sometimes, I get so invested in making positive change that I don't pace myself, and I can experience cycles of burnout. If you see me getting lost in my work, can you please help me monitor my energy and pace to maximize my impact in a way I can sustain?

→ My superpowers will 10X if you can help me identify the right people to help affect change, as well as help me identify other Catalysts who work like I do. Are you open to collaborating on building a Network Map for our project(s)?

→ Once we are at the point of implementing change, the repetition, focus on details, and potential resistance can be draining for me. I may need extra support during this period. Could we come together to brainstorm what this could look like to help me see possibilities?

→ At my core, I am a problem solver. If I come to you with a problem, please trust that I've already tried to address it myself and now need your help to identify a path forward. Can we find a way to troubleshoot these problems together?

→ Because I work in service of forward movement toward change instead of backward-looking documentation, I am not good at tracking success. When I forget to take a beat and celebrate my wins, can you help remind me of what I've already accomplished?

WORKING WITH ME 101

MY DEFINITIONAL TRAITS AND STRENGTHS

....

....

....

....

WHAT WILL HELP ME SUCCEED

....

....

....

....

GLOSSARY OF CONCEPTS

- **Action**—steps taken that move us toward our vision and provide information we can reflect and iterate upon.
- **Action Map**—a way to build action steps toward a vision; includes a starting point and an envisioned future state, with necessary possible steps to take (including rejuvenation practices) along the way.
- **Active Listening**—the skill of deeply focusing on the person speaking, understanding the information, and responding thoughtfully.
- **Articulating Value**—the ability to speak to the benefits and usefulness that our strengths can provide, in a way that matters to the listener and their needs.
- **Breadcrumbing**—the intentional act of helping people understand your path as you move through Vision + Action + Iteration to show how you got from A to B to Z; becomes a way to document your value and impact.
- **Burnout**—the experience of a one-way energy drain that leaves us feeling empty and exhausted; Catalysts experience burnout with frequency and intensity.
- **Catalyst**—a changemaker who takes in information across a wide range of inputs to come to visions of how

the world around them can be improved, feels compelled to move into action toward those visions, and inherently iterates and adapts the path to get there; related words include catalytic and catalyticness.

- **Catalyst Formula**—the process a Catalyst inherently uses to create change; Vision, Action, and Iteration, ideally encased within consistent rejuvenation, self-compassion and empathy for and community with others.
- **Celebration**—honoring accomplishments (sometimes including learnings and failure) that creates feelings of success and supports breadcrumbing; something Catalysts tend to do infrequently prioritizing forward progress rather than a sense of looking backward.
- **Empathy**—deep understanding of the feelings, thoughts, and experiences of another; for Catalysts, an awareness of the effect that our energy and the process of change has on others that redirects our actions to be considerate of their process, concerns, and needs along the journey we share with them.
- **Energy Tank**—a metaphoric tool used to bring awareness to our internal energy reserves, as well as the activities and practices that deplete or replenish it.
- **Iteration**—the adjustments and pivots we make to our actions and vision based on the ongoing feedback we're taking in.
- **Mania**—the frenetic "high" that we get while tackling a new challenge.
- **Mindfulness**—awareness that results from non-judgmentally paying attention, intentionally and in the moment; a tool that helps Catalysts slow down to more effectively create change and minimize burnout.
- **Network Map**—a way to plot out the actors we are working with and systems we're working within, identifying

endorsers, resistors, decision makers and influencers who participate in ideas coming to life; can also help us identify places of safety amidst resistance.

- **Not Right Now List**—a way to set aside the fresh ideas that we're not yet ready to focus on, so they don't feel lost but also don't turn into phantom goals.
- **Orchestration**—the actions required to "conduct the orchestra" of moving parts necessary to make a change come to life; the process of helping others see their role in achieving a shared vision.
- **Overcommunication**—the process of saying the same things over and over again in the process of orchestration; what feels like overcommunication to a Catalyst is often barely breaking through the consciousness of those around us.
- **Phantom Goals**—extraneous ideas; things we'd like to accomplish that are separate from the larger vision we're pursuing, that we unconsciously hold ourselves to achieving even when we aren't consciously focused on them.
- **Psychological Safety**—a state within a group of people where sharing new ideas or trying new things can be done without fear of negative consequences.
- **Prioritization Lists**—tasks aligned to your vision and Action Map that have been put in order by the most important to accomplish in the short term; once identified, tasks on the prioritization list should be put into our actual calendars to avoid them being phantom goals.
- **Purpose**—the reason we are pulled toward particular challenges and work; some people feel a capital-P Purpose that guides their choices across life; many of us use purpose to help us make choices about what change we'd like to make in the here and now.

- **Reflection**—an intentional pause after action to consider new information that came from that step before iterating.
- **Rejuvenation**—the intentional process of restoring and maintaining our energy via practices, including consistent routines, self-compassion, and a sense of empathy for and community with others; rejuvenation serves as the container of the Catalyst Formula, creating distance between ourselves and the work and lengthening the runway toward burnout.
- **Rejuvenation Routine**—consistent, intentional practices that create a sense of rejuvenation.
- **Self-Awareness**—the ability and willingness to view our own feelings and actions and the impact our feelings and actions are having on others.
- **Self-Compassion**—kindness directed toward yourself that creates room to learn, grow, experiment, and fail without internalizing messages of failure and shame.
- **Tours**—an ongoing act of orchestration that brings the network into our Vision, Action, and Iteration process to contribute to the solution and create buy-in for eventual implementation.
  - **Listening Tour**—intentional, active listening across the organization to better understand their context, concerns, needs, and success criteria.
  - **Co-Creation Tour**—bringing key players together to co-create a more targeted vision and plan of action toward it.
  - **Feedback Tour**—revisiting the broader map of individuals that we listened to in the beginning to catch them up on the vision and plan of action, get their stamp of approval, adjust any final major concerns, or simply inspire buy-in.

- **Trauma**—a spectrum of personal experience resulting from extreme mental or emotional stress or physical injury that triggers involuntary, instinctual responses in the nervous system; trauma can be acute, chronic, or complex, and while psychologists are learning more every day, it is increasingly clear that workplace trauma is both real and dangerous. Only you can know if you have experienced trauma. *Note: Trauma is not synonymous with PTSD, which must be diagnosed by a medical professional.*
- **Vision**—a clear view of an improved, potential future.
- **VUCA**—an acronym used to describe the increasing volatility, uncertainty, complexity, and ambiguity of the world and the situations we find ourselves in; Catalysts have skills that support our VUCA reality.
- **VUCA Prime**—a leadership model created by Robert Johansen to offset the four parts of VUCA with the positive responses of vision, understanding, clarity, and agility; skills that Catalysts possess.

ACKNOWLEDGMENTS

Thank you to Catalysts who participated in our research, building the foundation of our understanding today. You trusted us with your stories and pain, and the world is forever changed because of your willingness and courage to share. Special thanks to those who agreed to be interviewed for this book: Michael Bloxton, Anne Cocquyt, Hao Dinh, Donna Flynn, Chelsey Glasson, Virginia Hamilton, Justin Lokitz, Shakeya McDow, John Morley, Ashley Munday, Saidah Nash Carter, Georges Sassine, Breana Teubner, Van Ton-Quinlivan, and Alex Vaughn. All of your stories have made this book richer.

To the amazing Catalyst Constellations Advisory Board, Anne, John, Justin, and Shakeya, who first gently showed us the necessity of putting our research and tools into a book. For all of the inspiration your catalyticness has given and for all of the feedback and support you have provided along the way. Your generosity of time, spirit, and network have had a profound impact.

To Emily, thank you for dotting our Is and crossing our Ts and constantly trying to keep us from making HUGE mistakes due to how quickly we move and how few details we really pay attention to. Thank you for being our Chief Officer of Everything, strategy, technology, legal, finance, marketing, and soul support. When we talk to Catalysts about finding someone who "gets" you and can support your weak areas, we couldn't think of a better example.

To the fabulous Abby VanMuijen and Rogue Mark Studios. Thank you for bringing our words to life in visual form throughout this book. For all your support of the Catalyst movement. And for all the justice work you embody to make the world a fairer, better place. Thanks for pushing us to be better, more inclusive leaders.

To Jenn Harkness, thank you for bringing your brilliance and expertise to help us tackle the delicate topic of trauma.

Thanks to Meg Levie for the wisdom, support and jumping in, in typical Catalyst style.

SHANNON'S ACKNOWLEDGMENTS

To my Co-CEO, co-author and friend, Tracey Lovejoy. This book wouldn't exist if it weren't for your strong intuition combined with your amazing research skills, which created the foundation of the movement we are building. I am so thankful for your deep self-knowledge, incredible support as a partner, and tireless work ethic. You have shown me how to dream big, move into action, and manifest my dreams across all parts of my life, while minimizing burnout. Working with you brings constant joy and light into my life. I am living my best life because of you.

While the data is inconclusive about whether we are born or morph into becoming a Catalyst, I had the good fortune to have two Catalyst Moms, Brynna Kaulback and Rosemary Talmadge to show me the way. Through you I absorbed innovative ways to exist in the world (Future Search, Open Space, Appreciative Inquiry, Systems Thinking, Theory U, Proprioceptive Writing). Your lifelong passion and work to make a more beautiful, just, and inclusive world set the bar high. You taught me that our highest purpose is to help others. You taught me to be brave and reach out to the top. Mom, thanks for being in the car to pump me back up every time I got rejected selling Girl Scout Cookies. You and Nonni have shown me what a resilient, well-lived life looks like.

To my son Galileo, thank you for the patience you've had with your hyper-Catalyst mom. Whenever I got down, or had self-doubt, you have always been there to make me believe in myself again. Watching you turn into the amazing young man that you are is one of life's best gifts. I couldn't be prouder. Thanks for all the tech support. I love you more than all of outer space. And thank you for Betty.

Adam, my amazing husband, thank you for making the count-less meals for me while I was writing. I am so blessed to have such an amazing MAS club member and supporter in my life. I promise to consider having some plateaus on our life-long journey together. I love you with all my heart. You make everything better.

To all the Broadway boys in my life, I am so thankful to have you as family. You have made my life richer in so many ways. You fill my heart with love. I look forward to so many more adventures together.

To my dad, Ron Lucas, who introduced me at an early age to the things that sustain me today—getting lost in the woods and a Buddhist mindfulness practice. I am forever grateful for all the hikes you took me on, even if I didn't show it at the time.

Deepest thanks to my boo, Matt Morrisey, for a life-time friendship that has made me into the person I am. Thank you for our Fog Walks, sorting out the state of the world and our place in it. Sometimes, friends become family.

To my dearest friends Heather, Ellen, Maja and Karla, who are always there for me when I need them, who make me laugh, hold space for me to cry, who remind me of the truly important things in life.

To Brannan, who birthed/midwifed this book with us. Somehow the universe can give you the gift you didn't know you needed and weren't expecting. I do not know another soul who could have helped us realize our dream like you have. Tracey insisted we need a Catalyst and boy did we get one!

To my former bosses, who have helped me progress and strive to be my best self. To Juan-Jose Juan (JJ), for giving me the dream job and helping me to live outside the box. Thank you for showing me that work can and should be fun, risky, and have impact. You are always in my heart. To Kate O'Keeffe for showing me how important it is to step into my power and be big, and bold, and fearless. To Niklas Heuveldop for giving me the incredible opportunity at Ericsson. I am forever grateful for all the learnings and for the chance to spread my wings and fly.

Thanks to the rest of the Vodafone Innovation Family—Chris Brown, Joanna Dillon, and Francine Stevens—you never know what a motley crew can achieve when they act like family. Those were fun days, and I learned so much about creating positive change with you.

Thanks to those who have truly inspired me over the years. There are so many of you. I would particularly like to thank Beth Comstock for being a bad-ass Catalyst female role model. Often when I was tackling business/innovation problems, I would ask "What would Beth do?" You are an inspiration for female Catalysts, smashing the glass ceiling while creating massive positive change. And Peter Hinssen for your thought leadership, friendship, and fun. Thanks for introducing me to the CEO of Desks Near Me.

TRACEY'S ACKNOWLEDGEMENTS

To Shannon, my co-CEO, co-author, business partner, and dear friend, I never would have taken this step, nor be living my purpose so fully, without you. Gratitude feels like a small word when I think of what I feel toward you. Thank you for doing the deep work to build our partnership and the breathtakingly fun work to build our business. Thank you for the many gifts you bring like endless ideas, jumping at opportunities, supporting our technology and marketing, and bringing your full hyper-Catalyst self! We are building and growing because of the vision and action and iteration you bring to the Catalyst movement.

To Brannan Sirratt for being our partner in birthing this book—translating our research, experiences, and enthusiasm into something readable (lord knows if left up to my wordy, research speak the entire Catalyst population would be in a long slumber). Thank you for helping us see the power of the

Catalyst Formula as a container for the book and for Catalysts everywhere. And thank you for showing us how this content can shepherd a Catalyst's journey.

Thank you, Shane, my husband, life partner, and rock, for always seeing me as more than I've seen myself. I will always remember the star you put on our fridge in our first year of living together (way back in 1999) representing what you expected of my trajectory. It has given me confidence when I had none for myself. Thank you for guilt-free long nights so I could work on the book. Thank you for supporting and trusting me when I left corporate life. Thank you for building our life together.

Thank you to Sadie and Ryder for your grace each time I said I needed to push through another part of the book. Thank you for being proud of the work I do in the world and thank you for being the primary reason I would take breaks—for dog walks, long drives, Saoirse Ronan and Marvel movies, games of UNO and so much more—you are the best type of rejuvenation and best reason to practice mindfulness that ever existed. There is no greater honor in this world for me than being your mother.

Thank you Kiran Robertson for being my belly laughs and cry breaks and the primary reason I feel safety in this world. And thank you for bringing forward three of my favorite people in this world: Henry, Julian, and Ellis. Thank you for quarantining with us because life was on hold without having our households together. We did it—we built the life and family we dreamed!

Mom, thank you for the incredible gift of travel, which launched my curiosity about people and how their lived experiences shape them. And thank you for entertaining my big, broad questions about our existence from my earliest days.

Dad, thank you for shaping the researcher in me—developing my love for talking things out in structured ways and seeing them from a variety of perspectives and possibilities.

A thank you to Gayna Williams, who took a chance on me as a researcher coming right out of grad school and showed me the path into coaching and entrepreneurship. I wouldn't be living my purpose without your confidence in and guidance of me.

To the women who keep me afloat—Emily, Karen, Lauren, Lisa, Rachel, and Robin—every enquiry, call, text, and word of encouragement has provided me with love and energy that has kept me grounded and full during this process, and far before that! Thank you for being my biggest fans and being ready to help whatever the need or reason.

Finally, to Dr. Kelsey Klausmeyer—thank you for giving me the aha of the term Catalyst at that coffee shop at the beach all those years ago!

FROM TRACEY AND SHANNON

Thank you to Catalysts the world over that have shared their experiences and helped us see we were on to something important. And thank you for all the ways you push to make the world better for all of us and for generations to come. We know you will be solving our world's most wicked problems.

ABOUT THE AUTHORS

Shannon has been Executive Vice President at Ericsson, a Senior Innovation Architect at Cisco, and a Director of Innovation at Vodafone. A practitioner and global thought leader on intrapreneurship, she founded the Global Intrapreneur Salon and is passionate about transforming corporations into sustainable change engines.

Tracey is an anthropologist and the research engine for Catalyst Constellations. She spent twelve years at Microsoft leading teams of changemakers and co-founded the Ethnographic Praxis in Industry Conference. Tracey thrives when she can use her intuition and relentless optimism to coach Catalysts and amplify their changemaking power.

Milton Keynes UK
Ingram Content Group UK Ltd.
UKHW010731241123
433194UK00001B/88

9 781544 515779